HEROES *of* AMERICA ™

DANIEL BOONE

by **Roy Nemerson**

illustrations by **Pablo Marcos**

BARONET BOOKS, New York, New York

HEROES OF AMERICA™

Edited by
Joshua Hanft and Rochelle Larkin

HEROES OF AMERICA™ is a series of dramatized lives of great Americans especially written for younger readers. We have selected men and women whose accomplishments and achievements can inspire children to set high goals for themselves and work with all of us for a better tomorrow.

Table of Contents

Important Dates

1713   Squire Boone arrives in America from England

1734   Daniel Boone born in Exeter, Pennsylvania

1750   Daniel goes on first long hunt

1753   Boone family moves to North Carolina

1755   Daniel fights under General Braddock in French and Indian Wars

1756   Daniel marries Rebecca Bryan

1760   Daniel and family move to Virginia

1760–62   Daniel on long hunt in the Appalachians

1769–71   Daniel makes trip to Kentucky with John Findley

1773   Boone family moves to Kentucky; James Boone killed by Shawnees

1775   Boonesborough established

1778   Daniel captured by Shawnees; lives with them for over a year

1779   Daniel escapes from Shawnees; siege of Boonesborough

1782   Israel Boone, 22, killed in battle with Shawnees

1799   Boone family moves to Missouri

1810   Daniel Boone makes long hunt to the far West

1813   Rebecca Boone dies

1820   Daniel Boone dies

1845   Daniel and Rebecca reburied in Kentucky

Chapter 1

Born in America

Daniel Boone's destiny was set from the moment he was born. The late afternoon sun spread its light over the Boone family's log cabin on November 2, 1734, in the American colony of Pennsylvania, near a little town called Exeter. From her bed Sarah Boone, Daniel's mother, suddenly cried out in pain.

"Prepare hot water! Bring more blankets!" shouted one of the women in the room. She was a neighbor who had come to assist in Sarah's giving

"Prepare Hot Water!"

birth. Mothers gave birth at home in those days, and neighbors and family would come by to help. There weren't many doctors on the American frontier, and no hospitals.

Samuel Boone, Sarah's oldest son, ran out of the small cabin, and raced toward a little hut down by the riverbank.

"Pa, Pa!" Samuel yelled. "Come quick. Mama's havin' the baby!"

Squire Boone jumped up from his weaver's loom, and with his son, hurried back to the cabin.

Squire rushed to Sarah's side. Several women were helping to prepare Sarah for the birth.

"It'll be all right, Sarah," Squire assured his wife. He gripped her hand. Sarah let out one loud, piercing cry.

Then there was great joy in the room, for now another voice was crying—the cry of a newborn baby boy. One of the women wrapped baby Daniel in a small blanket and held him up for all to see.

Some who were there say, as baby Daniel cried and everyone cheered and clapped, that a remarkable thing happened.

A ray of the setting sunlight shone through the window, right on Daniel. The light bathed the baby in a reddish glow. Suddenly he opened his eyes and stopped crying.

Was it fate? Or destiny? The very first thing the newborn Daniel Boone saw was the sun in the west. From that moment on, and all his life, Daniel Boone's eyes would be looking to the western frontier; a frontier that he, more than anyone else, would help open up to all Americans.

But Daniel Boone's trailblazing frontier days were still many years ahead of him. The America he was born into was a lot different from the America of today. For one thing, America was still a colony of the British empire back then. All the

The Light Bathed the Baby.

people living in America were considered subjects of Great Britain, and the English king. America would not declare her independence and become a free nation until Daniel Boone was over forty years old. But the spirit of independence and rebellion was inside Daniel Boone long before 1776.

When Daniel's father Squire was 18, in the year 1713, he left England for America. Like thousands and thousands of others, Squire Boone came to America because it offered hope and a chance for a new beginning.

Squire, along with his parents, brothers and sisters, settled in the pleasant town of Exeter, about ten miles north of Philadelphia. This was natural for them because they were members of the Quaker religion, and many Quakers lived in this part of Pennsylvania.

The idea of family was very important to the Boones. They lived very close to each other. Each family member had his or her own land on which they built homes. The men all had regular jobs or trades, such as weaving or blacksmithing. Many of them hunted in the nearby woods. Pheasant, turkey, and deer made fine meals.

But they would also farm the land, especially with the help of the women. Keeping a farm was necessary in order to have food. It was critical in the winter months, when game hunting was very scarce.

So the world Daniel Boone was born into on that November afternoon was still a new world. It promised a new start. It presented the newcomers with opportunities; but it was a frontier. Much of America was still unexplored in the 1730s.

The greatest danger for the colonists involved the Native Americans, or Indians, as the colonists called them. The fact is, the colonists arriving in America were taking the Native Americans' land

A War For Over Two Hundred Years

away from them. Each new colonial settlement pushed them off their homeland. It was a form of warfare, a war that would continue for over two hundred years, before it was finally over.

Through these years many innocent people would be hurt and killed. The struggle over exploring and claiming new lands was the central struggle in Daniel Boone's life, but whether in time of war or peace, Daniel's relationship with the various tribes was special. That relationship further showed the greatness of Daniel Boone, and set an example for others to follow.

Of course, in Daniel's early boyhood years, thoughts of frontier trails, exploration and struggles were far away.

Even as a boy, young Daniel began to show the qualities that would one day shape his character and make others look up to him.

Daniel believed everyone should be treated

fairly. He showed this side of his character one afternoon when he was only eight years old.

One of the local boys was named Henry Miller. Like Daniel, he was eight. Daniel, Henry and a bunch of the other town boys were walking along the main dirt road that led into and out of Exeter. They were heading for the nearby woods, to see what game animals were about this early spring day.

"Since I'm the best woodsman among us, I'll lead the group," Henry Miller boasted.

"You're not the best," Daniel Boone replied. "You're just the loudest." The other boys found this funny and laughed. That got Henry Miller mad.

"Who you sayin's the best, then?" Henry demanded.

"You're lookin' at him, Henry," Daniel responded. And he stared square into Henry Miller's eyes, with the same stare he would be fix-

"You're Not the Best!"

ing on bears, cougars, enemy soldiers and unfriendly Indians in the years to come.

"I'm sayin' I'm the best, and until someone proves I ain't, that's the way it stays," Henry said.

"How do you want me to prove it?" Daniel asked. All the boys knew young Daniel Boone was the best shot in the county. Not with a gun—because these boys were too young to use guns yet—but with a slingshot Daniel had carved out of hickory wood. He could take three pheasants, four ducks and a possum between noon and sundown, any day of the week. He had the surest aim of any boy in the county, so Henry probably didn't want to challenge Daniel to a shooting contest.

Instead he pulled his arm back and quickly punched Daniel right across the mouth with his fist.

"Give up, Daniel Boone?" cried a triumphant Henry, laughing.

The blow had caught Daniel by surprise. He was on the ground, bleeding from the lip.

"Why don't you come down where I can see you, Henry?" Daniel replied. He reached out, grabbed Henry by the top of his leggings, and yanked him down to the ground.

As the other boys cheered them on, Daniel and Henry tussled, turning one another over, kicking and punching at each other. But soon Daniel got the upper hand. He was stronger than Henry and pinned the other boy to the ground.

Holding Henry's shoulders firmly, Daniel said, "I offer you the chance to submit, Henry."

This was the way people fought in America at that time. Once an opponent was down or beaten, he was offered a chance to surrender before further damage was done.

Knowing he had lost, Henry said, "I give up. You are the best." Smiling, Daniel got off Henry's

The Other Boys Whistled.

chest and let his opponent up. The other boys whistled and slapped Daniel on the back.

"Guess we know who's best around here!" one of the boys shouted.

"Guess we do," Daniel said, checking his lip. The bleeding had stopped and his straight, white teeth were fine. "So let's head off, we got some scouting to do. Henry, why don't you take the lead?"

There was stunned silence all around. No one could believe their ears, including Henry Miller.

"But Daniel, you beat me. I lost. You're the leader," Henry said, looking directly into Daniel's clear blue eyes.

"That's right, I'm the leader," Daniel said. "So I say Henry guides us through the woods. The leader has the right to make that choice."

Well, no one could argue with that. Daniel had made a decision, and the group would follow it. But this incident showed that even as a young boy,

DANIEL BOONE

Daniel Boone had qualities that would serve him well in the years to come.

Everyone had seen Daniel beat Henry Miller. He saw no value in rubbing it in. To have kept Henry down after that would only make them enemies. This was a chance to show Henry, and the others, that he could put differences behind him and treat others with dignity. It was an example of the spirit that made the new American frontier and its people so special—and it came naturally to Daniel Boone.

"What I've learned out in the world, they don't teach you in the schoolroom," Daniel was heard to say much later. Daniel's frontier learning came from his real life experiences. His formal education was very limited. But his knowledge was great.

Quickly, Daniel and Henry Miller became very best friends. Henry wanted to be a weaver, and so Daniel's father took Henry in as an apprentice.

Daniel and Henry Miller Became Best Friends.

DANIEL BOONE

This meant Henry lived in the Boone home while he studied and learned his trade under Daniel's father.

Daniel Boone's apprenticeship, at a very young age, was to learn how to survive on his own on the frontier. He would become one of the greatest frontiersman in American history.

Chapter 2

First Steps On The Trail

"Come on, you critters, get a move on, move now!" Daniel shouted.

In 1747 Daniel was almost thirteen years old. Sarah Boone went to the family dairy farm several weeks a year to tend to the cows, and she brought Daniel with her to help. Since it was summer, Squire Boone gave Henry a week off from his apprenticing to join Daniel at the farm.

Daniel glanced up at the clear Pennsylvania sky. It was late afternoon. "Sun will be setting 'fore

"Come On, You Critters!"

too long," Daniel said. "Can't hunt after dark."

"Hunt?" echoed Henry, frowning. "Who's going to hunt?"

"I am," Daniel replied, "and if you promise to keep a proper silence while we're in the woods, you can join me."

Henry laughed. "In the woods? How do you plan to do that when we have no shooting rifle?"

Daniel smiled at his friend. "Help me get the last of these cows in the barn and I might show you something."

The boys got the herd safely in. Daniel pulled the door shut and bolted it. It took great physical strength to do that. But though still only a boy, Daniel had a broad, strong chest and arms. People in the county said that Daniel Boone could out-muscle a man twice his age.

"Race you down to the dairy!" Daniel shouted.

The two boys took off, running down the dirt

road that led to the bottom of the hill.

"Can't beat Daniel Boone!" Daniel roared as h
touched the dairy first, a good five seconds ahead o
Henry.

"Ah, quit your bragging and show me the thing
you were telling me about," Henry said.

Daniel led him out back. Henry saw a blanke
on the ground. Daniel bent down and lifted it up
Underneath it lay a brand new, shiny American
long rifle.

"A long rifle!" Henry said, his voice filled with
awe. "Where did you get that?"

"My father gave it to me, right before we came
here," Daniel said. He picked up the rifle and held
it near his chest.

Henry stared at the weapon. The American
long rifle was the finest gun of its kind in the world
It was made by European immigrants who settled
in Pennsylvania and Delaware. With this gun, the

"A Long Rifle!"

colonists could kill all the game they needed for food. The long rifle was also used to drive the Native Americans off their land when they didn't leave peaceably.

"Your father must trust you mightily," Henry said.

"With a rifle, yes," Daniel replied. Squire Boone had to stay back at the family house in Exeter with the other Boone children, to attend to business. Although the dairy farm and the homestead were only a few miles apart, Sarah and Daniel would sometimes be away for several weeks at a time.

"My father knows I'm a crack shot," Daniel said. "Giving me the rifle, he knows we'll be safer here, if anything should happen."

"Have you tested it in the woods yet?" an eager Henry asked.

"Not yet," said Daniel.

"Then let's go!" Henry replied, tugging on

Daniel's hunter shirt.

"All right, but I've got to tell my mother first."

Sarah Boone was inside the dairy. She looked up as the boys entered.

"Mother, the cows are in the pen, so Henry and I thought we'd visit the woods a while, to see if any game's about."

Sarah Boone's face clouded over. Like Daniel, she had fine, long, straight black hair. But unlike her son, her eyes were a dark, intense brown.

"It'll be dark soon, Daniel. I don't want you about in the woods after sunset. No telling what's out there."

"We'll be back before dark, mother, I'll have a pheasant with me for supper."

"I fancy more your coming home safe," she said. "But if you should get a pheasant, that would be fine. Now get a move on before it gets dark."

The boys headed off, down the dirt road toward

"We'll Be Back Before Dark."

the woods.

"Pheasant *would* be nice," Henry said as they turned off the road and entered the thick woods.

Daniel glared at his friend. "Why not say it a little louder so all the animals in the next county can hear you?"

"Sorry," Henry responded in a near-whisper. "But these woods aren't like the ones back near town. They're so much thicker and bigger. I've not seen anything like this."

"That's 'cause they haven't been civilized yet," Daniel whispered. "Outside of this one little path, no human hand's touched these woods. They're just the way God made 'em. And that's how it should be."

"Wonder who made this path," Henry said as they continued venturing into the thick dark forest.

"Shawnees, most likely," Daniel said casually.

Henry let out a little gasp. "You don't think

we'll see any out here, do you?" he asked nervously.

"Might. Never can tell who you're gonna meet up with in the woods," Daniel replied. "Now hush up and keep your eyes open."

A good many tribes lived along the eastern Pennsylvania frontier in the 1740's. It wouldn't be another ten years until a major war broke out between them and the new Americans. But already there were some incidents where tribes and settlers had fought.

Walking along the path, Daniel and Henry suddenly came to a rise. The path opened up. Lying before them was a huge valley, filled with more woodlands. A river could be seen in the distance, and farther west, the Allegheny mountains.

Henry looked out at the valley and whistled softly. "What a beautiful sight that is!"

"I agree," said Daniel. But he was looking elsewhere. He had his rifle cocked, and was aiming

"What a Beautiful Sight!"

directly overhead. He fired rapidly three times. A moment later, a huge pheasant fell into a bush just a few feet away.

Daniel grabbed the dead bird out of the bush, and held it up.

"Yahoo!" he said. "Won't that make a fine supper!"

Henry was impressed. But he was also nervous. It was getting darker, the sun setting behind those mountains in the west.

"Maybe we should start heading back, Daniel."

Daniel paused for a moment. His eyes grew narrow, his square jaw set firm. "That might take a little longer than we'd planned," he said finally.

"Why is that, friend?" Henry inquired.

In reply, Daniel nodded and glanced over Henry's shoulder. Henry turned around. Heading toward them was a party of over half a dozen Indians. Some had tomahawks and rifles in hand.

"Daniel, run, or we're dead boys!" Henry yelled.

DANIEL BOONE

But Daniel knew the worst thing they could do now was run. And besides, as the group got closer, he recognized one of them, a boy about his own age, named Little Wolf. Daniel realized this was Little Wolf's family; his father, mother, brothers, sisters and perhaps a cousin or two.

"Daniel, run, while we still have a chance!" Henry cried. He fled into the woods.

Daniel, however, said nothing, but kept watching the approaching Shawnees.

In moments, they were face-to-face with Daniel.

The tribes of Pennsylvania spoke some English, having learned it over many years of trading with the settlers. So Daniel spoke to them.

"Greetings to my friend Little Wolf," Daniel said.

"Daniel Boone, you are always a friend of ours," Little Wolf replied. Daniel was well-known among

"We Can No Longer Live Here."

them. They had seen and heard of his great ability with his little handmade wooden slingshot.

"I see you have a rifle now," Little Wolf said.

"It is only for hunting wild game," Daniel said.

Little Wolf nodded, indicating he realized Daniel intended them no harm.

"It would seem the family of Little Wolf is making a trip," Daniel said. He looked at all the Shawnees, and nodded to each. They nodded back in return.

"Yes," said Little Wolf. His eyes seemed to mist slightly. "We are making a trip. A very long trip. We are leaving this land. My father says we can no longer live here. The settlers have taken too much from us. We can no longer stay."

"But where will you go?" asked Daniel.

Little Wolf's father, White River, stepped forward. He was a short man, but strong in build. He stared hard at Daniel. "West," said White River.

"Our future is in the West, where we shall live again in peace with the land, as is our birthright."

Then White River nodded to the others in the group, and they continued to walk along the path.

Daniel stood to the side, watching as they passed him. He felt sad for them that they had to leave, but he also felt a twinge of envy. Once again, young Daniel Boone's mind was filled with thoughts of the great unknown West, the land of wonders where millions of buffalo, bears, cougars, coyotes, turkeys and other sorts of animals ran freely, where there were more rivers than a man could count and mountains so tall, so huge, that their tops had snow on them all the year round.

Daniel turned to watch the last of the family cross over the rise, and disappear down the other side, heading for the valley below. Heading west. And as Daniel watched them, the last rays of the setting sun shone on him, and bathed him in red.

A Twinge of Envy

Chapter 3

The Hunting Life

"Look at him. Lord, he's gotta be six feet at the shoulder. He'll feed the family for a month or more!" Daniel whispered to Henry.

"Get him 'fore he decides to walk off, Daniel," Henry said.

"Shh, I know what to do," Daniel replied as he carefully loaded his long rifle.

The two boys were watching a black bear as it lazed against a rock near a small stream in the woods. Daniel was now 15 years old. Over the past

40

couple of years he had hunted every chance he got. Daniel had won fame far and wide as one of the best rifle-shots in all of Pennsylvania.

A black bear was a rare sight these days. With the land around Exeter being cleared and developed by thousands of new settlers, many of the large animals, like bear and deer, had disappeared. Daniel wanted to be sure not to lose this huge beast. He aimed, lined up his sights, and fired.

"You got 'im, Daniel! Yahoo!" Henry shouted as he leaped up and scampered down toward the stream.

Henry laid out some ropes so they could haul the bear back to the Boone homestead.

Daniel looked down at the bear. Its paws were half as large as a man's chest, its teeth long and sharp.

"C'mon, gimme a hand here, Daniel," Henry said, as he began roping the bear. "Hey, where're

"That Makes It Official."

you going?"

"Just a minute," Daniel said, going to a nearby sycamore tree. He took out his long hunting knife and into the bark he carved the words, "Danl Boone kild a bar here 1750."

"Okay," Daniel said, when he had finished. "That makes it official."

It wasn't the last time Daniel Boone would carve his bear-killing exploits into trees in the wilderness. There are stories that over the next fifty years, hunters and pioneers found Daniel Boone's name carved into trees all across the American frontier, from the mountains of Pennsylvania to the far west.

"I can't wait to see their faces when they see this beauty," Daniel said, meaning his parents and brothers and sisters, who now numbered seven.

"Probably gonna be the best supper party in

the history of Exeter!" Henry declared.

The boys reached the Boones' house. Daniel's father and mother were talking by the front door.

"Ma! Pa! Look here, I brought you a little present!" Daniel called out.

His parents turned and stared at him. One look told Daniel that something was happening. "What is it?" he asked.

"Son, we're going to be moving," Squire said.

"Moving?" said Daniel. He stopped in his tracks and dropped the rope. "Where to?"

"This is a big country. We need more space. We'll find a new home, don't you worry," Squire said.

"But what about me!" Henry wailed. "My apprenticing isn't done yet. What'll I do?"

"I spoke to your parents, Henry," Squire said, "and they've given you permission to come with us. You must promise to return at least once a year to

"Son, We're Moving!"

visit them, and all will be right."

So it was that several weeks later the Boone family, with Henry included, loaded all their goods into three Conestoga wagons and began the journey to search for a new home.

Daniel was chosen to be the guide, scouting ahead as they made their way into the frontier wilderness.

"The roads are said to be good along this route," Daniel told his father as they started off. "Being the month of May, the weather should be fine. I think we can make at least fifteen miles a day."

Daniel was right. The road, known as the Allegheny Trail, was a good one. Then, about the second week out, it took them around a curve, and suddenly Daniel looked up in wonder.

"Mountains!" Daniel gasped. "Look at those mountains!"

"Those are the Appalachians, son," Squire Boone said.

"Can we cross them, Pa?"

"No, that way heads west," Squire said. "We're taking the path that leads down to Virginia."

"But, Pa, let's go west!" Daniel cried.

"No, not for us, not now. Come along, Daniel."

Squire Boone called out for the wagons to continue on their way. What thoughts could have run through young Daniel's head as he looked for the first time at those mountains, the gateway to the unknown western lands of America? He knew he wouldn't be crossing them now. But he knew he would someday. They would meet again.

The journey lasted about a month, and the Boone family settled down in Linnville Creek, just over the border in the colony of Virginia. The land was good for farming. With all the Boone children there, plus the husband and wife of the two who'd

One Last Hug

married, there were more than enough hands available to do the farming.

So Daniel convinced his parents that he was ready to go on his first "long hunt," with Henry as his partner. A long hunt meant going out hunting for several weeks or months at a time. The purpose was to kill as much game as possible, then to sell it for as much money as possible. The longer the hunt, the more money could be made.

The morning arrived for the boys to head off. It was the first time Daniel would be away from home for more than one night. He couldn't wait to be on his way.

With one last hug from his mother, Daniel bid the family good-bye. He and Henry headed out into the great unknown Virginia wilderness. Daniel had two long rifles with him; he'd be in charge of the hunting. Henry had the traps, which they'd be setting for beavers and otters. Beavers were especially valuable, as women liked beaver fur for their hats and collars.

The boys were filled with high spirits as they set out. They first went into the nearby Shenandoah Mountains. There were stories of ten-foot-tall bears and giant mountain lions in this forest. After five days, however, the largest animal they'd spotted was a squirrel, which they killed only so they wouldn't go hungry that night.

"The hunting in Exeter was better than this," Henry complained. The boys had moved on now further south, toward the Blue Ridge Mountains, near the Virginia-North Carolina border.

"It's gonna rain bear'n beaver real soon. I can sense it in my bones," Daniel said.

"Well, no insult to your bones," Henry replied, "but so far it's only rainin' squirrel and rabbits, and that's a pretty poor rain."

Suddenly the horses reared up and came to a

"It's Gonna Rain Bear'n'Beaver."

sharp halt.

"Quiet now," Daniel said softly. He slipped off his horse and pulled a long rifle from its holder. "You keep the horses quiet on the road. I'll take a look about."

Daniel crept silently into the darkened woods on his left. The horses had shied away from that direction, so it likely meant there was something in there.

Daniel started through the thick brush. There were trees everywhere. There was no clear path. Each step could be taking him closer to mortal danger, Daniel knew, but also closer to a great prize.

Daniel paused to glance around. There seemed to be no streams or clearings in sight. Bears usually tended to gather at such places. But all was quiet. There were no bears in this area. So what had made the horses react so?

Daniel looked up to see how much daylight he

had left. And it was then he saw it.

A cougar was sitting on the limb of a tree about seven feet above Daniel's head. He was growling softly, and his large brown eyes were staring right at Daniel.

If Daniel didn't act now, it would be all over for him. As the cougar rose to leap and strike, Daniel quickly pulled his rifle up, aimed, and fired.

"What was that?" Henry yelled from back on the road. He came running through the brush. He saw Daniel bending down, inspecting the dead cat. Daniel's bullet had hit the cougar right between the eyes, while the cat had been in midair, heading right for him.

"Jehosophat!" Henry exclaimed.

"Nope," said Daniel. "Just an old cougar." And with the coolness he always would display in such situations, Daniel began to cut the cat into sections, to load into a salt basket for preserving.

The Cougar Rose to Leap and Strike.

DANIEL BOONE

For the next seven weeks, Daniel and Henry hunted and trapped all along the beautiful Blue Ridge. By late October they had over fifty large animal furs, including bear, beaver, otter, deer and, of course, one cougar.

"What do we do now?" Henry asked. Their horses nearly groaned under the weight the boys were loading on them.

"Now we head up to Philadelphia and sell to the highest bidder," Daniel replied.

And sell them they did. The money the boys got for their skins was the most they'd ever seen in their lives by far—nearly $500. And in America in 1750, $500 was equal to most people's yearly income.

Henry was excited. "We have $500, Daniel. We're rich!"

"Only one thing money's good for, Henry," Daniel replied.

"What's that?" Henry asked.

"Spending!" Daniel said. And with that he led the two of them on a spree through Philadelphia. They ate the best food, drank some wine, bought clothes, stayed at fancy hotels. Two weeks later, the $500 was completely gone.

"Wasn't that a time, friend?" Daniel asked, as the two boys were finally ready to return to Linn-ville and the Boone family home.

"Never seen anything like it," Henry replied. But other than that, Henry said nothing else until the two boys reached home in Virginia.

They'd been away for nearly three months, and the family was overjoyed to see them again. Daniel had great fun telling them about their hunting and trapping adventures, and then their experience in Philadelphia.

"Can't wait for the spring so we can do it again!" Daniel beamed.

Away for Nearly Three Months

Although he had loved the hunting trip, Daniel had to admit it was nice to be back in his old familiar bed. He lay in the glow of a candle the first night back, thinking of how glorious the past few months had been.

There came a knock on his door.

"Come in," Daniel said.

Henry entered the room. He looked quiet and thoughtful.

"Henry, what is it? What's the matter, friend? You've been quiet and gloomy ever since we left Philadelphia."

"Daniel, I enjoyed the hunt. And I know you'll be heading out on many more. But I'm afraid it's not for me."

"What? Why are you saying this?" Daniel sat up straight.

"It's just the way I am," Henry replied. "I need something safer in my life. I'm planning to be a weaver. That's who I am. Being a hunter, that's who you are. I also can't bear the thought of spending all that hard earned money so fast. A man should save some for a rainy day, you know."

Daniel knew there was no use arguing with Henry. A man either was born for the hunting life, or he wasn't. Spending the money was part of the adventure. For there would always be a next hunt, and it would bring more money.

But if Henry wanted no more of it, Daniel knew he couldn't force him.

"I understand, Henry," Daniel said.

The two friends shook hands. Henry turned and left the room.

It had been the first and only time they would go hunting together. About a year later Henry moved out to start a weaving business of his own. They never saw each other again.

"I Understand, Henry."

Chapter 4

War Comes To The Frontier

The move to Virginia was good for Daniel. His days were filled between helping with the farming at home, and going off on hunting trips into the woods.

As things improved for them, Squire Boone moved the family again, this time to North Carolina, to a region called Yadkin Valley.

Here Daniel found even more plentiful game to hunt. It was said that one autumn, Daniel Boone killed ninety-nine bears.

But Daniel pursued animals not only because he loved to hunt. Daniel learned early that hunting could be a good livelihood. And for all his life, hunting would be Daniel Boone's main source of income.

"There are three things a man needs to be happy," Daniel was fond of saying. "A good gun, a good horse, and a good family."

In Yadkin Valley at this point in his life, Daniel Boone had all three. By now he was the oldest of the Boone children still living with his parents. Four of his brothers and sisters had married and moved into nearby farms of their own.

But young Daniel, now in his late teens, was not yet ready to settle down.

His energy and spirit were a perfect match for this growing new frontier land.

His hunting won him the reputation of being one of the best marksmen in North Carolina, just as it had wherever he'd lived.

Energy and Spirit

DANIEL BOONE

By now, in the mid-1750s, the struggle for land between colonists and Native Americans was becoming violent.

Frustrated that they were being forced off their homelands and driven farther away by the settlers, the Native Americans became allies of the French. This was because the French were enemies of the British. So it was the Indians and French against the British and Americans, who were British colonists.

With the French and Indians on one side, and the British and colonists on the other, it wasn't long before war came. It would be known in history as the French and Indian War. And it was young Daniel Boone's introduction to warfare.

The war officially began in 1755 when Daniel was 20 years old.

It would decide whether the French or the British would get all the land from western Pennsylvania clear across to California. It would also decide, in time, what the fate of the Native Americans would be.

For Daniel there was no question of what he had to do. He had no arguments with the Indians, but he felt loyalty for his fellow colonists and he disliked the French, whom he considered intruders.

The French came down from Canada and set up a fort near Pittsburgh, in Pennsylvania.

The British had to destroy this fort, for it was on a river that led the way west. If the French held this ground, it would stop the British from moving west.

So the British, under the command of General Edward Braddock, planned to attack the fort, and chase the French back north into Canada.

In North Carolina, under Major Edward Dobbs, a unit of local frontiersmen was formed to fight with Gen. Braddock. Daniel Boone joined this

The French Set Up a Fort.

unit. Daniel's official title was teamster, which meant he was with the horse patrol. His job was to make sure the horses were always ready, healthy, and prepared for combat.

"I've never been to war myself, son," Squire Boone told Daniel on the morning of his departure. "But I know if you do the kind of job you're capable of doing, then you'll come out just fine. And we're all proud of you."

The Boone family, with all the marriages of Daniel's brothers and sisters, had grown very large now. Daniel had at least a dozen nephews and nieces, so his leaving for war had many in tears.

But Daniel put all those thoughts behind him as he marched off with the other volunteers. Within a week they had met up with Braddock's forces. They numbered over 2,000 men, and it became Daniel's job to help cut through the narrow path that led north, so that the great cannons could make their way through the forests.

It took nearly two months, but by July 9, 1755, the men finally reached the mighty Monongahela River. Less than a mile up this river the French had their fort, atop a high hill.

"Men, prepare to cross!" Gen. Braddock called out. The British regular soldiers, in their redcoats, and the American colonist soldiers, dressed in blue, holding their rifles aloft, went across the river.

Daniel looked around. It was a dazzling sight. So many soldiers, all perfectly drilled and trained, with fine weapons.

But just as he had once felt the presence of that cougar in his bones, Daniel suddenly knew something wasn't right.

Daniel turned to one of the officers. "Sir, I think we shouldn't stay too long in this place. We're in the lowlands, and the fort's at the top. It makes us good targets."

"Prepare to Cross!"

The British officer smiled at Daniel. Did this raw, young, uneducated American think he knew better than the British officers how to conduct military affairs? He was about to scold Daniel when suddenly shots rang out.

"We're under attack!" shouted one of the North Carolina volunteers.

In moments, warriors appeared all along the hillside, rifles in hand, and began firing at them. At the same time, French-Canadian soldiers raced down from the fort, and with rifles and small cannons, blocked the road. The British and Americans were trapped. They couldn't escape!

"We're surrounded!" desperately shouted one of the Americans.

Now there was panic, as men fired their rifles in every direction.

The Americans, who had fought in these woods before, ran to fire from the safety of the trees. But the British troops had never seen anything like this before. They were new here. They knew only one way to fight: stand your ground, and fire.

"We've got to get these horses back across the river to safety!" Daniel yelled to one of the other teamsters. All around them bullets were flying. Men and horses were being shot and killed.

"Our orders are to stand here and fight," a young American officer said to Daniel. "We must obey orders."

"Yes, sir," Daniel replied. It wasn't until days later that Daniel learned that the officer's name was George Washington.

Meanwhile, soldiers were being killed by the hundreds. Finally, when General Braddock himself was hit and fell to the ground, the Americans felt they were no longer under his orders.

The rampaging Indians were screaming bloody war chants. They were scalping the dead and shoot-

"Don't Feel Like Dyin' Today!"

ing the living. The French continued to fire at the British and Americans from the safety of the hill.

Daniel knew his only hope would be to flee on horseback. He cut the harness of a horse tied to a wagon and jumped on.

An Indian leaped at Daniel, his tomahawk just grazing Daniel's shoulder.

"Don't feel like dyin' today, friend," Daniel said, as he kicked out at his attacker. Then, with gunfire and smoke and bloodshed all around him, Daniel galloped off, back across the river.

For Daniel Boone, his first taste of war was a shock. His horse soon grew lame, and Daniel had to leave it. He made his way back toward home on foot. As he approached Yadkin Valley and was about to cross the Juniata River, a large Indian with a bottle of rum in his hand suddenly leaped out of the bushes and screamed at Daniel.

"Your life is over now, Long Rifle!" the Indian

bellowed. Daniel no longer had a long rifle or any other weapon. All he had were the shirt and breeches he was wearing, and the moccasins on his feet.

Daniel had no spirit in him now to fight. "Just let me be. I want no trouble," he said.

"No more trouble?" the Indian laughed. "Not after you're dead!"

Daniel saw there would be no way around fighting this drunken man. He thought of all the young men he'd just seen slaughtered on the Monongahela. Suddenly Daniel was filled with a fury he didn't know he possessed.

"Then one of us dies!" Daniel yelled, and he charged at the Indian. He struck the man squarely in the gut. With his great strength, Daniel lifted him under the arms and threw him over the side of the bridge.

The man screamed and landed forty feet below, in the river.

He Struck the Man.

It was said that Daniel Boone was a major Indian killer. But the fact is, in his entire life, Daniel killed exactly three Native Americans. For Daniel didn't have the *war* spirit in him. He had the *life* spirit.

Killing another man gave him no joy. He silently, slowly continued on his way home. When he got there he told his family about the disaster that had befallen Braddock's men. But he never told them the story of the Juniata River bridge.

Daniel Boone saw no glory in that.

Chapter 5

Rebecca

Returning home from the bloody battle, Daniel decided he'd seen enough of war for a while.

The Boone family, which was constantly growing larger as more and more of Squire and Sarah's children married, was prospering in both farming and land management. They had become important citizens of Yadkin Valley.

Daniel spent the rest of the summer of 1755 helping with farm chores and, of course, going off and doing his hunting.

"Why Don't You Stop By?"

But Daniel was nearly 21 years old now. Even some of his younger brothers and sisters were already married. Daniel hadn't thought about marriage at all up until then.

But he soon realized that "a good gun, a good horse, and a good family" meant more than just your parents and siblings. Family might also mean a man's wife and their children.

Daniel often went hunting with the Bryan boys, who were neighbors of the Boones.

"Our family's havin' a bear roastin' tonight," Sam Bryan said one day to Daniel. "Why don't you stop by? It'll be a good one."

Daniel had a fat turkey in his gun sight. "Maybe I might," he said as he fired, and a heartbeat later had another turkey to add to his day's catch.

Daniel didn't notice when Sam smiled and winked at his two brothers. They had plans for

Daniel Boone that Daniel could never have guessed at.

What Daniel did not know was that the Bryan boys' sister Rebecca had asked them to invite Daniel to the gathering. Rebecca was 17 years old, and with her long, flowing dark hair and deep brown eyes, was considered one of the prettiest girls in Yadkin Valley.

All the boys wanted to dance and flirt with Rebecca. All except one. Daniel Boone.

"That rascal would rather flirt with his rifle," Rebecca complained to her brother Sam. The fact was that Daniel, for all his spirited ways, was on the shy side when it came to girls and socializing.

It wasn't that Daniel didn't like girls. It had to do with how he'd grown up. He'd barely had any formal schooling. While other boys and girls were learning and playing together, young Daniel had been out in the woods, often alone, just him and

All the Boys Wanted to Dance With Rebecca.

his long rifle.

So Daniel didn't know all the proper social ways to behave around girls. Rebecca Bryan was going to teach him.

That night at the roast, a fiddler band played mountain music. People danced, ate, drank. Everyone was having a really good time.

Almost everyone. Daniel sat up against a fence, just watching all the goings-on.

"Daniel Boone, why are you sittin' out here all alone?"

Daniel turned. Rebecca Bryan was standing in front of him. She wore a pretty white dress and her eyes sparkled in the firelight.

"Wanna see a trick?" was all a bashful Daniel could think to say, and before Rebecca could answer, Daniel pulled his knife out and tossed it in the air. He was going to catch it and twirl it around a few times, to impress Rebecca.

But being nervous, Daniel's aim was off. "Watch out!" he shouted, as the knife flew out of his hand, and headed right toward Rebecca.

Startled, Rebecca jumped out of the way. The knife missed her. But it came down right along the skirt of her long dress. The sharp knife cut a gash almost a foot long, right down the side of the dress, before jamming into the ground, and pinning the bottom of Rebecca's dress with it.

Daniel stared at the knife. Rebecca stared at Daniel.

Daniel carefully removed the knife and without saying a word jumped up and ran off, his cheeks red with embarrassment. Rebecca just watched him go, and shook her head. Then she started to laugh.

The next day, at home, Rebecca was telling her family about the bashful Daniel Boone, when there came a knock on the front door. Rebecca went and

She Kissed Him on the Cheek.

opened it.

Standing there was Daniel Boone. He smiled nervously.

"Howdy," said Daniel.

"Howdy," said Rebecca.

Daniel cleared his throat. "I brought you somethin'. To make up for the, well, for, you know, last night," Daniel stammered.

Rebecca laughed. "You don't have to make up for anything, Daniel Boone. But what'd you bring me?"

"Actually it's for your whole family." Daniel pointed up the path. A freshly killed deer lay on the ground.

Rebecca was delighted. "We'll have it for dinner!" she squealed. "You're a darling, Daniel, and you're invited to join us!" She kissed him on the cheek.

Daniel stammered a little, and then said,

"Well, I'd better get it butchered up. You can't eat i
like that."

Daniel took the deer out back, preparing it for
cooking. Rebecca and her mother and sisters were
busy inside, readying the dinner table and the fire
place.

Two hours later Daniel knocked on the front
door again.

Rebecca opened it. Daniel had the deer meat
all neatly cut and quartered, ready for cooking.

"Here 'tis," Daniel said, handing the basket of
meat to Rebecca. "Could I come in for a cool drink?"

"Why, of course, Daniel," Rebecca replied. She
stared at Daniel as he entered the house. All of
Rebecca's sisters stared at Daniel. Rebecca's
mother stared at Daniel. They watched him as he
drank cup after cup of cool cider.

What they couldn't take their eyes off were
Daniel's shirt and breeches. They were bloody red

She Stared at Daniel.

from the butchering he had just done. He hadn't thought to bring another shirt with him, to change into. He never did at his own home.

At Daniel's house, such a thing would go unnoticed. But the Bryans considered themselves to be socially above most people in Yadkin Valley.

Certainly no one had ever sat at their dinner table before in a bloody shirt.

At first Daniel didn't realize what all the giggling was about. But he quickly caught on. In his own way, he got even.

As he lifted a wooden noggin to take a drink, Daniel paused. He looked at the noggin. "Why, this noggin's like my shirt," he said. "Looks like it could use a good washing."

This made everyone laugh. Daniel showed he understood they disapproved of his bloody shirt at the dinner table. But he also showed Rebecca he could make jokes, too. They would make a good match after all.

And so it was on August 14, 1756 that Daniel and Rebecca were married. In fact, it was a triple wedding, as two of Rebecca's cousins married two of Daniel's cousins. The Boones and the Bryans were creating a large, extended clan.

By 1760 he and Rebecca had two sons, James and Israel. They were living in their own home, a small farm near a town in North Carolina.

Daniel built them a log house. It was big, with a separate kitchen area, firm floors, and a huge fireplace.

More children were born, and Rebecca tended to their rearing. At the same time, she saw to the cooking and cleaning and helped with the farming. She was a good shot too, and very brave at handling firearms.

Daniel had to keep making money to provide for his growing family. He earned some doing black-

A Band of Cherokee Warriors

smith work and teamster work.

But mostly he earned money by hunting and trapping, for North Carolina was filled with game of all types. Often Daniel would go off on a long hunt for weeks at a time.

For all his domestic happiness, Daniel could never forget that the French and Indian War was not very far away. On a day in 1760, the war again came close to Daniel. This time it almost cost him his entire family.

A band of Cherokee warriors, armed by the French, made a series of raids along the coast of North Carolina.

News of the raids reached Daniel. By now he and Rebecca had three small children. A daughter, Susannah, had been born that February.

"We'd best move into the nearby army fort until the threat is over," Daniel said. The family packed up and was taken into the safety of Fort Dobbs.

After several weeks, it was reported the Cherokees had moved on.

Daniel and Rebecca returned home with their children. What they found there saddened them greatly.

Some of Daniel's neighbors had decided to stay. Their dead bodies were found everywhere. Then the Boones reached their own home. Most of the cabin had been destroyed, and a lot of the farmland had been burned.

"What'll we do?" Rebecca cried, staring at the destruction.

Daniel put one arm around his wife, and with his other held his small children.

"We'll do what we have to do," Daniel said. "We'll move on."

Daniel moved the family north, into Virginia. They settled in Culpeper County and were joined by Daniel's parents, two brothers and a sister.

"We'll Move On."

It was while hunting in the Virginia backlands one day that Daniel met a man who would change his life.

The man's name was Burrell. He was an African-American slave who had worked as a cowherd for a settler in the back country. Burrell told Daniel there was hunting and trapping land to the west, over the Blue Ridge Mountains, unlike anything he'd ever seen.

"Buffaloes for as far as your eye can see! So many beavers they practically choke the river streams! And bears! My lord, so many bears!"

"This is the news I've been waiting to hear," exclaimed Daniel.

He was now nearly 25 years old. If he was ever going west, it had to be now.

That night Daniel told Rebecca his plans, a long hunt to the west, which might last several months.

Rebecca was a strong woman. In the past few years she had seen and lived through much. But the thought of Daniel leaving, being alone in the wilderness for many months, filled her with sadness and some fear.

"There's enough game here, Daniel, why must you go looking for more somewhere far away?"

How could Daniel explain it? In words, he probably couldn't. But already he was feeling closed in, in this Virginia county. The call of the western frontier was something he had to answer. And perhaps if Rebecca had seen Daniel as a baby, bathed in the red western sunlight, she'd have understood.

But Rebecca realized there was no stopping her husband.

"I'll return. Safe. And with money, because what I kill and trap in the west will make us rich for a lifetime," Daniel promised.

So there was yet another tearful farewell, and

The Best Hunter

DANIEL BOONE

Daniel Boone again left his home, headed for the Appalachian Mountains, and the path west, wherever that led. He had only his horse, two dogs, and three long rifles with him. For him, that was enough. He was Daniel Boone.

Following Burrell's directions, it took Daniel only a little over a month to reach the summit of Whitetop Mountain in southern Virginia. From here he could see the hills and valleys of the Appalachian forest. It took his breath away.

He spent most of the autumn hunting and trapping in what today are national forests in North Carolina and eastern Tennessee.

Daniel's reputation as the best hunter and trapper in the area grew quickly. Daniel believed he was a good hunter because he was a good farmer. He knew all the trees and plants, by sight as well as name, so he knew which animals would be feeding on them, and when.

He became so good, that in the Tennesse
mountains, if someone was called a "Boone",
meant he was a good hunter.

Daniel had some encounters with Cherokees o
the trip. More than once he was surrounded b
their hunting parties. Daniel never showed fear i
their presence. They respected him for that.

But while they didn't harm Daniel, they di
take his furs and supplies.

"You are hunting on our lands. These are ou
goods," they would say.

Daniel would shrug and go hunting and trap
ping anew. This made his trip last much longe
than he'd expected.

By the time Daniel felt he had earned suffi
cient money for his efforts, his long hunt int
Appalachia had extended nearly two years.

When Daniel finally returned home, a tearfu
Rebecca held him with her head pressed to hi

Surrounded by Hunting Parties

chest for nearly five minutes. She couldn't even speak a word. She had been convinced Daniel had been killed and she was never going to see him again.

"Sweetheart, I told you not to worry. I'd come home and bring money with me," Daniel said, holding up a pouch of gold coins.

"I have something to show you as well, Daniel," Rebecca said. She went into the house, and came out holding a little girl. Rebecca had given birth while Daniel was away. They now had four children. A big family.

"But you're home. And that's all that counts. We're a family again," Rebecca said, again putting her arms around Daniel's neck.

Daniel held his wife close. He said nothing. But on the hunt, while in Tennessee, he had met a man who had told him of even greater hunting grounds in land farther to the west.

DANIEL BOONE

So even as he hugged Rebecca, and as his children came running up to greet him, and he held his new daughter, Daniel was thinking about this new land. It was called Kentucky. Daniel knew before long he would have to go there.

John Findley

Chapter 6

I'm Goin' To Kentucky

"Daniel Boone! Daniel Boone live here?"

"Good lord, who could that be?" Rebecca asked as the Boone family was finishing breakfast.

Young James Boone, Daniel's oldest son, ran to the front door and looked outside.

"It's a man in a funny hat, Pa. He's ridin' a white horse."

From the description his son gave, Daniel Boone knew this could be only one man, John Findley. Daniel had first met Findley when they had been teamsters together, fighting under General Braddock back in 1755. They had met again when Daniel had gone hunting in the Appalachians. Findley had told Daniel about Kentucky. Daniel had invited him to come visit if he ever got to Virginia. Six months had passed since that day, but Findley had made it.

"Welcome, John Findley!" Daniel boomed out.

"It's good to see you, lad!" Findley replied, hopping off his horse.

Findley had been born in Ireland, and he had come to America as a boy. He had red, flushed cheeks, a broad, friendly smile, and eyes that danced like a mountain stream.

"Just in time for a little breakfast," Daniel said. He showed Findley into the house.

"Family, I want you to meet a good ol' friend of mine," Daniel announced. "John Findley. He's the greatest hunter in the whole territory."

"A Good Ol' Friend"

DANIEL BOONE

"Next to your pa!" Findley roared, winking at the Boone children. By now Findley was seated at the table. Rebecca was setting plates of bacon strips, eggs, breads and corn grits in front of him, and Findley was eating them up as fast as she put them down.

"Daniel, tomorrow's May first. If you're ever gonna go, now's the time," Findley said, finishing off his last buttered biscuit.

"Go?" said Rebecca, clearing off the table. "Go where?"

Daniel frowned. He'd been reluctant to tell Rebecca about his dream of going to Kentucky. He knew she wouldn't like the idea of his going off again for such a long time. He understood that. But he knew it was something he had to do, and that ultimately it would be good for the whole family.

"Why, we're goin' to Kentucky!" Findley beamed, sitting back in his chair. He patted his well

106

fed stomach. "Gonna git us all the fur and hides to make us rich as kings!"

Daniel quickly got Findley out of the house, and the two men went for a hike in the nearby woods.

But that night, after the children and Findley had gone off to sleep, Rebecca spoke to Daniel.

"Daniel, you can't go off again. Last time it was nearly two years you were away. It's not right. You don't get to see your children grow up. And I get so scared," Rebecca said.

Rebecca was a strong frontier woman. Daniel knew she wasn't scared for herself, but for him. He needed to reassure her he was doing the right thing.

"Rebecca, we've got a large family now. I need to make a better living for all of us. Kentucky can provide that. More than that. It can make us rich."

"We don't need to be rich," Rebecca said. "We've

"Isn't That Enough?"

always had enough. You've got a loving wife, wonderful children, a good home, a nice little farm. Isn't that enough?"

Daniel paused. Again, he had trouble finding the right words. How could he ever explain what went through his soul when he heard the very word "Kentucky"?

"Rebecca," Daniel said softly. "There are many ways a man can be rich. I've been blessed. I have the best family a man could ask for. But there's something else. Something I need to do, like I was born to do it. My goin' west is as natural as a bird takin' wing or the fish takin' to the stream or the deer takin' to the woods."

"Or the Cherokees taking your scalp," Rebecca said, grimly.

Daniel stood up and put his arms around his wife. "Don't you worry. Only person who's cut this dark hair o' mine these past years has been you.

And that's not gonna change."

Rebecca knew there was no keeping Danie from going west. She understood it was his life' dream, and she didn't want to spoil that dream Reluctantly, she gave him her blessings to make the trip.

"We'll be back 'fore the leaves turn red," Johr Findley boomed out the next morning. Helped b; Rebecca and the children, Daniel and Findley hac finished packing their horses.

The men had enough provisions, equipmen and ammunition to last them through the end o summer.

There was a tearful parting, and then Danie and Findley were on their way west. To Kentucky.

"What we're lookin' for is The Great Warrior' Path," Findley said.

"That's the trail that'll lead through the Cum berland Gap and into Kentucky?" Daniel asked.

A Tearful Parting

"Yes, sir," Findley replied. The two men were now camped for the night. The light from the camp-fire danced across their faces. Daniel paused as somewhere nearby an owl let out a low hooting sound.

"Hope we don't have any trouble with Chero-kees," Daniel said. "Had enough of that my last hunt."

"Don't you worry," Findley said, laughing. "Only trouble yer gonna have on this trip is countin' all the money we're gonna make!"

Daniel and Findley continued west. It was hard going, and the men barely spoke, to save their energy.

But after nearly two weeks out, Daniel was getting concerned.

There was still no sign of this Great Warrior's Path. Daniel was beginning to fear that Findley's great land of Kentucky might not really exist.

"Have faith, friend Daniel," Findley kept saying. "Have faith."

"I have loads of faith," Daniel said, "I just wish we had a good map."

The words were no sooner out of Daniel's mouth than the two men approached the top of a rise in the road. And suddenly, spread out before them, as far as the eye could see, were rows upon rows of rolling blue-green hills. And beyond these, even more.

"I've never seen hills that color," Daniel whispered in admiration.

"That's 'cause you've never seen Kentucky before," Findley replied. "But now ya are!"

"What are those dark things moving below?" Daniel asked.

Findley peered down and he smiled. "Them's buffs, Daniel. They're miles away, but all those little shapes moving out there are genuine American

Thousands of Them

buffaloes!"

Daniel was awed. There must have been thousands and thousands of them! The stories were right. Kentucky *was* the promised land.

"Well, let's get down there!" Daniel said. At last his eyes sparkled and his smile came easily. It was first time in his life that Daniel Boone was in the territory of Kentucky. But he felt as if he had come home.

Daniel and Findley met up with some of Findley's hunting companions. They set up a base camp, and from there went out hunting. Sometimes they'd be away for days at a time. They'd return with their catch, which others in the camp would then skin or prepare for packing and eventual selling.

"Buffalo, elk, deer, beaver, otter, bear, wolf!" Findley cried as he and Daniel returned to the camp with their latest spoils. "Few more months of this and we'll never need to hunt or work again,

Daniel Boone!"

Daniel stretched his legs out by the warm fire. The month was now December. It had turned into a very long hunt. They had promised Rebecca that Daniel would be home by autumn. But that was not to be.

"Perhaps we have enough for this trip," Daniel said. "We must have over 500 pelts and furs by now."

"Daniel, before long this territory will be as crowded as Virginia and the Carolinas," said John Stewart, who was one of the other hunters. Stewart was also Daniel's brother-in-law, married to Daniel's younger sister, Hannah. "This could be our only and best chance to cash in on Kentucky, while we have it practically to ourselves."

Daniel agreed. He was feeling uneasy again, but he pushed those thoughts out of his mind the next morning as he and Stewart set out to hunt

500 Pelts and Furs

upstream.

Suddenly a group of braves came rushing out of the woods.

"Stop there!" cried one of them. His name was Will, and he was the leader. Quickly the braves had Daniel and Stewart surrounded.

"We're goners," Stewart whispered to Daniel.

"No, just take it easy," Daniel whispered back. He'd been in such situations before.

"Greetings," Daniel said. "I'm Daniel, this here is John Stewart. Who would you be?"

"We are Shawnee. My name is Captain Will. You are hunting on our grounds!" roared the leader.

"Well, seems to me there's plenty of land around here for everyone to hunt," Daniel said. "After all, how much can me'n my buddy here catch, anyway?"

"I have heard of you," Will said. "You are the one who wears the tall hat and shoots the long rifle.

DANIEL BOONE

You kill and take many hides from the Shawnee ground!"

Daniel was known not only by his reputation as a hunter. Unlike the other American woodsmen, he didn't wear a coonskin cap. Daniel hated the furry headpiece, and wore a traditional hat. This made him easy to recognize as he rode and hunted through the wilderness.

"There's a treaty with the Iroquois, and it gives us the right to hunt in these parts," Stewart said.

"We do not recognize the Iroquois treaties!" yelled Captain Will. "This is Shawnee land, not Iroquois land! Take us to your campground where your skins are. Now! Or we will kill you!"

"They Won't Hurt Us."

Chapter 7

The Hard Frontier

It was nearing sundown when they approached the camp.

"What'll they do with us once they have the skins?" Stewart whispered to Daniel.

"They say they won't hurt us. I choose to believe them," Daniel replied.

"Why?" asked Stewart.

"Because I don't want to consider the alternative," Daniel whispered back.

Stewart knew what Daniel meant. Daniel

began clearing his throat and coughing.

"What's the matter, Long Rifle?" asked Captain Will, pulling his horse up to Daniel's. "Are you sick?"

"Guess so. Been out in this wilderness too long I reckon."

Daniel glanced at Stewart and winked at him quickly. Stewart realized what Daniel was doing. The coughing and throat noises were signals the frontiersmen used. It was like an alarm bell. If someone was coming through the woods coughing and such, it meant trouble. That was a signal to the others to get away as quickly as possible.

A few moments later they reached the camp site.

"It worked!" Stewart whispered to Daniel. Indeed it had. Findley and the other camp members were gone, as were their horses. But in their rush to go, they had left all the valuable furs, hides and

An Alarm

skins in the camp.

"They forgot to take the goods," Daniel moaned softly.

Instantly, the Shawnees, under Captain Will's direction, gathered up all the pelts and loaded them onto their horses.

"Good hunting, Long Rifle. You have done your job very well!" Will laughed. Then with a swooping motion, he ordered his warriors to race off into the woods, taking all of the furs with them.

Daniel and Stewart had not been harmed. But everything they had caught, the hundreds of furs and pelts and hides, were gone.

Stewart felt like crying. "What do we do now?" he said.

"Start over," Daniel said. "It's winter. Best time for the beaver catch. And we haven't a moment to waste."

Findley and the others were too dejected by the

Indian raid, and had ridden back east for the winter. John Findley would never return to Kentucky. Daniel would never see him again.

With no time to lose, Daniel and Stewart set out to trap the valuable beavers.

They returned to their campsite one early evening, with their horses holding the pelts of fifteen beavers.

"It's good we stayed on, Daniel," Stewart said. "We're starting to recover a lot of our losses."

"Hold it!" Daniel said suddenly.

"What?" said Stewart, concerned.

"Our camp's right around that bend. Look, there's smoke. Someone's started a fire." Daniel took out his rifle. Stewart did the same.

They got off their horses carefully and approached cautiously.

As Daniel peered through some bushes into the camp, he smiled.

"Just a Brother Boone"

DANIEL BOONE

"What is it?" Stewart asked. "Not more Shawnees?"

"Nope," said Daniel, standing up. "No Shawnees. Just a brother Boone."

It was Daniel's baby brother, Squire, Jr., who had come to Kentucky with a friend, Al Neely. The two brothers held a happy reunion.

The next morning Squire and Neely stayed at camp. Daniel and Stewart set out to trap more beaver.

It was now the late winter of 1770. Daniel had been away from home for over a year. The two men decided to split up. Daniel would stay on one side of the river, while Stewart crossed to check on the beaver trap line on the other side. Stewart got onto their wooden raft. Daniel started off toward the line upstream.

Suddenly there was a great shout. "Help! Help!"

Daniel spun around. The raft had hit a large rock in the river, and had split into pieces. Stewart clung to a wooden shaft as the rapids carried him off downstream.

"Jump off, swim ashore!" Daniel shouted out.

But the roar of the rapids became too loud. Suddenly John Stewart disappeared. At that moment Daniel remembered that Stewart had once told him he didn't know how to swim.

"Oh lord, no!" Daniel cried out. He ran down the side of the river, looking for any sign of his brother-in-law. He kept running alongside the river for hours. But there was no sign of Stewart.

A year or two later, a frontiersman would tell Daniel that a skeleton of a man near some broken wooden shafts had been found way down river.

But that day, Daniel Boone found nothing. All he knew was that John Stewart, not just a relative, but one of his best friends, was gone. And there was

John Stewart Disappeared.

nothing he could do about it.

When he told Squire and Neely what had happened, they both were greatly upset.

"This is a real dangerous, uncertain land," Neely said. "I'm not sure I belong here."

"Quitter!" yelled Squire Boone at his friend.

"No, Squire," said Daniel. "Each man has to decide where he belongs in this world. No one can tell you where that is but yourself."

"It's cruel out here!" Neely wailed. "If the Indians don't get you, then the river will! Or a bear! Or the freezing cold!"

"It's a world where a man has to keep his thoughts about him," Daniel said. "But as for cruel, I've seen much cruelty in so-called civilized places, sometimes far crueler than out here."

"I think I'll take my chances with that so-called civilized place," Neely said, throwing his sack onto his horse. "I'm sorry, Squire. I really am. But I want to go home."

"I understand," said Daniel's brother. "And look at it this way. Fifty years from now, when people talk about the first settlers in the great Kentucky territory, you'll be able to say you were there."

"But didn't stay," Neely said, lowering his head.

"Lift your head up, son," Daniel said. "You got nothing to be ashamed of. And keep your head up. You're gonna need it that way to spot trouble on the way back."

Neely nodded grimly, and soon he was off.

"Looks like it's just us Boones now," Squire said.

"Maybe that's how it was supposed to be," said Daniel. He squeezed his brother's shoulder. But his thoughts that night were never far from poor John Stewart.

For the rest of the winter, Daniel and Squire hunted together in the great Kentucky territory.

Squire Would Return.

They were the only settlers among all the tribes in the area. Each day could bring harm or death, either through the force of nature's wilderness, or an encounter with the Shawnees.

"We have had a fine winter," Daniel said, as spring of 1771 approached.

"We have shivered, suffered, nearly starved at times, almost been captured on several occasions, and you call it a fine winter?" Squire nearly shouted at his older brother.

"Why, yes," replied Daniel calmly. "We have endured, and we have been with the great natural world. Happiness comes from that knowledge within, as much as what you gain from it on the outside."

And the outside wasn't bad. At this point, the brothers had several hundred dollars' worth of beaver skins, ready to be sent for trading. They decided that Squire would return to the settlements with the pelts, would sell them and give some of the money to Rebecca. Then Squire would return to Daniel with additional supplies, so they could hunt and trap into the spring and summer.

And so it was that Daniel Boone was finally alone in the Kentucky wilderness, as Squire headed off.

What went through his mind during these weeks he was alone we shall never know, for there was no one there to record it.

But it is reported that a small hunting party was making its way through Kentucky at that time. As the hunters neared a clearing, they heard a mighty yelling.

The hunters quietly crept up toward the clearing. When they reached it, they were amazed by what they saw.

Lying on his back, rolling a little on the ground, was Daniel Boone. He was singing at the top of his

Singing About Mountains and Freedom

voice, a song about the mountains and freedom.

During this period, nothing disturbed Daniel Boone. He lived in caves when it rained, caught whatever food he needed to eat to survive, studied the many leaves and grasses and berries, so that he came to know each by sight, no matter where he might be.

Sometimes he would think of Rebecca and his children, and he would suddenly become sad. But with his horse and a few dogs that were still with him, he would fight off the sadness.

It was during this period alone that Daniel learned the things that would make him the greatest frontiersman in American history. But probably Daniel never thought of it as the "frontier." He thought of it as home.

More than three months had passed when Squire finally returned.

"Good to see you, brother!" were the first words

out of Daniel's mouth. And, he realized, these were the first words he had uttered to anyone since Squire had left.

"Good to see you, Daniel," Squire replied. "They miss you at home, and they hope to see you soon."

"They will," Daniel replied, unloading the supplies. "One more good season of hunting, and we'll have earned enough to go home."

By the end of the fourth month, they had over seven hundred dollars' worth of furs and hides strapped to their horses.

"We have enough," Daniel said. "We can go home now."

They began the trip back to The Great Warrior's Path, which would lead them out of Kentucky, and back east.

Their final night before reaching the Path, Daniel and Squire camped out by the roadside.

"We Can Go Home Now."

"I told Rebecca I'd be away just a few months," Daniel said. "It's been nearly two years."

"I think she realizes by now what being married to Daniel Boone means," Squire replied, smiling.

Suddenly, swiftly, their little camp was overrun by Indians. Squire froze with fear, but Daniel, as always, remained calm. As the Indians shouted and screamed, and ran around the campfire, Daniel opened up his arms and held out his hands.

"Sit with us," Daniel said. "We need not be enemies."

These were Cherokees, not Shawnees, and they did not know of Daniel Boone. But their leader, Tall Wind, liked Daniel instantly.

The Indians sat around the campfire with the two Boone brothers. They drank cider; they shared a pipe of tobacco.

All was friendly, all was happiness. At last it

came time for the Cherokees to move on.

"Thank you for being so kind," said Tall Wind.

"It is the way all men should be," Daniel replied.

"Agreed," said the Indian leader. "So you will not mind if we take your furs and hides from you."

"I would mind very much," Daniel replied.

"Then I shall have to insist on it," the chief said. Quickly the hides were cut off the Boones' horses and transferred to the Cherokees' steeds.

Daniel and Squire jumped up, and started to go after the ones doing the cutting.

Instantly, the Boones were surrounded by Cherokees, with knives drawn.

"Let it be," Daniel said to Squire. The Boones watched helplessly as the Cherokees rode off with their furs.

"If you hadn't sent me back with that first supply of furs, we'd have lost everything," Squire said.

Surrounded by Cherokees

"We have our lives. We have our strength. We have our families. We have tomorrow," Daniel said. "We don't lose everything even if we lose all the furs. We will return someday and reclaim what is ours."

Two days later, Daniel Boone rode his horse back into his hometown in Virginia. It was a mild evening, in May 1771. Daniel had left in May, 1769.

In all that time, Daniel had not trimmed his hair or beard, and his clothing looked just as raggedy.

"Wonder if Rebecca will even know me," Daniel said, as he and Squire approached the homestead.

"Look, they're over yonder, at the neighbors' place," Squire said, pointing.

Music and laughter rang out. The neighbors were having a hoe-down of some sort. There were a lot of people around.

Daniel saw Rebecca instantly. She was by a

cooking stand, talking to another woman.

Daniel approached slowly. He came up behind Rebecca and tapped her on the shoulder. She turned around. "Yes?" she asked, looking at the sloppy, shaggy man.

"May I have this dance?" Daniel asked softly.

"I must refuse, sir!" Rebecca replied, barely able to conceal her disgust at this dirty-looking man.

"But why refuse?" Daniel asked. "You have danced with me many a time."

And slowly Rebecca turned back and stared at Daniel. Recognition filled her eyes. She began to cry.

She screamed and threw herself into Daniel's arms.

Daniel laughed softly as he held his wife. She buried her head against his shoulder, and they slowly danced to the music.

Dancing With a Ragged Stranger

DANIEL BOONE

The people standing around, watching them, all wondered why Rebecca Boone was dancing with this ragged stranger.

But before long word spread that Daniel Boone was back from the Kentucky frontier. People gathered around as Daniel spent the rest of the evening telling them all about the west. About the animals, the Indians, the land. But mostly, about the wonder of it all, and the sheer beauty of the great frontier.

Chapter 8

Massacre In The Forest

Bend. Pick. Drop it in the basket. Bend. Pick. Drop it in the basket. It was going through Daniel's brain like a steady beat.

He was sweating freely. He was wearing only his shirt top and breech pants, but it didn't make him any cooler. Picking corn in the midday July sun was hot work.

Then Daniel looked across the road. Less than a quarter mile away, neighbors were picking corn in their fields. Neighbors, who you could see, picking corn right next to your own farm! Daniel never thought he'd see such a thing. People weren't meant to live this close together.

Daniel wondered if it was cooler in Kentucky, with those blue hills and rolling streams, streams you could dive into and refresh your body and soul all at once.

How sweet it would be coming home in Kentucky, knowing you weren't surrounded by people, closing in, crowding you in. In Kentucky there was land and room, and a man could breathe free.

It had been a few years since Daniel had returned from his Kentucky adventure. Rebecca had gotten him to promise that he'd stay home to help with the family farm. Rebecca had recently had their seventh child, and then their eighth. Daniel couldn't leave Rebecca at such a time. He had to stay. He was forced to do all his hunting around Yadkin now.

"No Place to Raise This Family."

DANIEL BOONE

That is, what little hunting he could still do. The area had become so populated these last few years, most of the game had long since moved to other areas. Daniel could barely keep the cupboard filled with good meat.

Daniel glanced again at young James filling his basket with the green corn. And something in Daniel Boone couldn't take it anymore.

"That's it, we're moving," Daniel said, striding into the house. Rebecca was holding the newborn baby boy, Jesse, in her arms.

"Moving? What do you mean, Daniel?" Rebecca asked.

"I mean this is no proper place for us to be raising this family," Daniel replied. He was pacing the room as he spoke, waving his hands excitedly, very unusual for him. "It's too crowded, there's too little hunting, too little money, not enough land. We need to move on."

"And where would you suggest?" Rebecca asked. She knew what the answer would be.

"Kentucky," said Daniel.

"Kentucky's still a wilderness, Daniel. It'd be too dangerous to take the children to live there," Rebecca replied.

"I've been talking to some of the men in town. The Russells are willing to go if we do. Others might come along, too. I'm sorry, Rebecca. I can't live like this anymore."

"If that's what you think is best, then I say let's do it," she said softly. Daniel couldn't believe his ears. They were going to move to Kentucky! So on September 25, 1773, the Boones and several other families gathered their belongings into their wagons and made ready for the trip. In all, the group numbered around fifty, including the children.

"Are we ever coming back here, Papa?" asked Levina, Daniel's little seven year old daughter,

The Group Numbered Around Fifty.

starting to cry.

"I don't think so, angel," Daniel replied softly. "We're goin' far away."

But little Levina kept crying. Many others also shed tears, for both the travelers and those staying behind knew this would probably be the last time they would ever see each other. And with many an eye still red, the group began its journey toward its new home. Beyond the hills. Beyond the valley. With Daniel Boone leading them all.

As the group camped down after a day of difficult travel, Daniel approached his oldest son, James.

"We're gonna need more provisions if we're gonna make it to Kentucky before winter, James," Daniel said.

"Just tell me what you need, Father," James replied. The boy, who was now 16, had his father's strong chin and clear eyes. And, most importantly, he had his father's broad shoulders, strong arms, and strong character.

"I need you and two of the other boys to go to Carolina and get us more provisions. Once you have the goods, you can meet us by the Warrior's Path entrance."

With a firm handshake, James took leave of his father. He was joined by two Mendinall brothers.

The next day the moving party made only five miles. The path was getting narrower. It was becoming more difficult to get the wagons through.

"We may have to ditch the wagons," Daniel said to Russell.

"How can we do that?" Russell asked.

"We'll strap the provisions to the backs of the horses," Daniel replied. "We'll make faster time that way."

"Sounds dangerous, Dan," Russell said, slowly shaking his head.

"Massacre, Massacre!"

DANIEL BOONE

"This is the frontier we're heading into, Russell," Daniel said. "If you don't want to take chances, maybe it's not the place for you."

At that very moment a young man came racing up to the camp.

"Massacre, massacre! Indians have massacred some people, just a few miles up the trail!" the young man screamed.

Daniel Boone grabbed the young man, and pulled him from his horse. "No need to scare the whole territory, you little fool!" Daniel said, glaring into the man's eyes. "Now where did this massacre happen?"

" 'Bout five miles straight down yonder," said the man, pointing. "There was at least three of 'em, their bodies all slashed, scalps missin', it's awful."

Daniel paused. "Three of them?" he said softly. Daniel turned to Russell. "Hold the camp, get the rifles loaded, keep everyone calm."

155

"Where're *you* goin'?" Russell asked, as Daniel leapt onto a horse.

"I'll be back 'fore sunset," Daniel said. Before he rode off, Daniel looked across the way. Rebecca was staring at him. There was a look of concern on her face. Daniel turned away, gave his horse a kick. and was off.

It took Daniel less than half an hour to reach the massacre site. Several hunters who had happened by were standing around.

Daniel jumped off his horse and approached one of the men.

"There's been a massacre here?" Daniel asked.

"One of the worst I've seen," the man replied.

"Where are the bodies?" Daniel asked quietly.

"They're wrapped in those sheets over there," the man said. "But I don't think you want to see 'em. They're cut pretty bad."

Daniel turned. It was clear from the shapes

"Wrapped in Those Sheets."

that one sheet contained two bodies, the other sheet just one.

Daniel bent down and carefully folded back the sheet with the one body in it.

"Oh lord, no," Daniel moaned softly. He recognized the body of his son, James.

"What have I done? James, James, forgive me!" Daniel cried. He bowed his head and pressed it against his son's cold, bloody brow. And Daniel Boone began to sob.

News of the massacre of James Boone and the two Mendinall boys alarmed all the settlers and colonists in the area. It meant the Shawnees were once again on the attack. The wilderness was once again a place of great danger.

It made most of the people traveling with Daniel's party turn around and return to their homes. The journey to Kentucky was over.

But Daniel Boone would not retreat. James

Boone was buried in a simple grave near the site where he was killed. As Rebecca and the remaining Boone children cried and held each other, Daniel approached James's simple grave.

"I promise we'll finish what we began, son. I promise we will yet make it to the promised land of Kentucky. I will do this, in your name. And if I do not, then know that I will die trying."

His eyes red, his throat choking, Daniel laid a single flower on his young son's grave.

Unwilling to return to Virginia but not yet ready to venture toward Kentucky, Daniel settled the family in Clinch Valley, North Carolina. It was near the Appalachian Mountains, not far from the massacre site.

The family lived in a small cabin in the woods. Daniel was able to hunt, but farming was not possible on this land.

"Daniel, we cannot stay here," Rebecca

Richard Henderson

pleaded. "There is no future for the children here. We must move."

"Not back to Virginia," Daniel said. "You know what my plan is. I made a graveside vow to James. I aim to keep it."

"But how?" asked Rebecca. "We can't go to Kentucky by ourselves. We need help and support. And we're not going to find it here in this little cabin in the middle of nowhere!"

Rebecca was right. They wouldn't find help or support. But it somehow managed to find them.

It came in the form of a visit to their cabin one day in early 1775 by Richard Henderson.

"Mr. Boone, I am president of the largest land purchasing company in the entire western territories," he said, when he arrived on horseback, with several other men.

"I've got no land for you to purchase," Daniel said.

Henderson smiled and nodded. "No, but you've got something very important to offer. Mr. Boone, your reputation as the finest tracker and hunter is known to all. Rumor has it you've even hunted and trailblazed in Kentucky."

"I did, year or two back," Daniel replied. He felt uneasy with men like Henderson. Daniel liked people who lived on, for, and by the land. People like Henderson saw the land only as property, to be bought and sold. They rarely saw the beauty of the land itself.

But Henderson said something to make Daniel sit up and take notice. "Mr. Boone, I'm making you an offer. We need to build a fort on the Kentucky River. This fort is important, because it can control the gateway to the West. We, the settlers, not the Shawnees or Iroquois, will control the frontier. I want you to lead a group of men to make a large clearing through the wilderness trail to Kentucky.

"Mr. Boone, I Am Making You an Offer."

When you reach this spot, you and your group will build the fort. The Kentucky and Detroit militias will then follow that trail and occupy the fort.

"In exchange, once you've completed this task, we will give you free land in Kentucky, which your family can move to and live on for the rest of your lives."

"But what about the Indians?" asked Rebecca, alarmed at this proposal. "Isn't the danger great on the frontier?"

"We've made land deals with the Shawnees and Cherokees," Henderson replied. "No more Indian wars. The land is yours, if you're willing and able to blaze the trail."

Daniel stared at Rebecca. She looked away. Daniel knew she was leaving it up to him. This was his greatest dream, and that it was now being offered to him filled Daniel with great emotion.

Daniel slowly rose to his feet. "Mr. Henderson,

I'm not much good at doin' business or makin' deals," Daniel said. "But I know when I hear somethin' I like. And I like the sound of this very much. You got yourself a deal."

The two men shook hands. Everyone in the room cheered and clapped, except for Rebecca. She stared at Daniel. She'd already buried one son in the name of frontier exploring. She had made a silent vow to herself that such a thing would never happen again.

As Daniel received the congratulations of all the men present, Rebecca knew that her vow would be put to a great test in the days to come.

Blazing the Great Trail

Chapter 9

They've Got My Daughter

With Daniel in the lead, nearly eighty men set out for Kentucky in March, 1775, to blaze the great trail.

Once that goal had been reached, Daniel would return for his family, and lead them to their new home in Kentucky. But first much work needed to be done.

With long swords and shears, they had to clear a wide path through the Appalachian wilderness. The trail would have to be easy to follow for those coming after them.

"Hey, hey, keep choppin', men!" Daniel found himself yelling many times a day. He was concerned. He knew the men were eager to reach Kentucky and reserve the land each had been promised by Henderson.

But Daniel knew it was important to clear this path properly. Their very lives might depend on it.

"Friends, I know you're in a hurry to reach Kentucky. So'm I. But remember this. The path we're clearin' is for soldiers to follow after us. Soldiers will be protectin' us, our wives, our children. Without a good path to follow, those soldiers might never get through. Think on that, while you're doin' your clearing."

The men took in Daniel's words and began working with renewed energy. Daniel Boone was an inspiring leader.

By April, they finally reached the spot on the

"Keep Choppin', Men."

Kentucky River that had been marked for building the fort. In Daniel's honor, the area was officially named Boonesborough.

Later that night, the men celebrated their arrival. There was much playing of music and drinking of cider. Daniel was concerned. They were in a remote wilderness. Although Henderson had said the local tribes had signed treaties, Daniel knew that agreements on paper didn't always mean that much on the frontier.

"We need to have some men standing watch," Daniel said to one of the other men. "We're defenseless like this, making all this noise."

"Daniel, you're a brilliant trailblazer and fine hunter, but you've got to learn how to relax and enjoy yourself a little!" one man said, as he took another swig from his jug.

Daniel knew how to relax and enjoy himself. But with the memory of James's death never far from his thoughts, he knew this was definitely *not* the way to do it.

Suddenly there were loud voices from the far side of the camp.

"Come quick, there's a man bleedin' bad!" someone shouted, as Daniel raced to the scene.

A man was face down in the dirt. Deep in his back was a tomahawk.

The men gathered around. Silence fell over the entire camp. Daniel pulled the tomahawk from the dead man's back. He held up the bloody weapon for all to see.

"That's Cherokee," Daniel said. "That's their way of welcomin' us to Kentucky. Now do you believe me when I say we must be on guard at all times? This land is still filled with danger. Only by staying together and staying organized will we be safe."

It was a lesson each man there would never

"War's Comin', War's Comin'"

forget. But it didn't mean they would always be safe. Safety was still many years away.

In May of 1755, Daniel felt the fort was well enough underway for him to return for Rebecca and the children.

On his way home, Daniel camped one night near the Tennessee border. A young boy came riding up on horseback.

"War's comin'! War's comin'!" the young boy shouted.

"Hold on there, what's that you say?" asked Daniel.

"American soldiers last month fought against the British at Lexington and Concord, in the colony of Massachusetts, sir!" the boy reported. "War of Independence has begun!"

Daniel nodded and the boy went on his way. So the war for independence from Great Britain was finally here. It meant America might soon be a new country. He stared into the fire. Independence. Freedom. They were just words to most men. To Daniel, they had been a way of life. He hoped all his fellow Americans might soon know the feeling—not just the word!

In September, 1775, Daniel was back in Boonesborough with Rebecca and the children.

By now, many others had returned with their families. A number of bachelors and single women had also come to the settlement to begin new lives. All together, there were now over 200 people in Boonesborough.

It wasn't long before Daniel's brother, Squire, Jr., arrived with his wife and family. Boonesborough was soon a small but thriving little settlement on the Kentucky River.

But until those lands could be cleared and homes built on them, Daniel never stopped warning the new settlers about the need to keep alert,

Beginning New Lives

within the safety of Boonesborough and the nearby fort, now under the control of American soldiers.

"This is a land of great beauty," Daniel told those who would listen. "But there's nothing beautiful if you're six feet under the ground."

Daniel especially went out of his way to say this to members of his own family. The one who needed to hear it the most was Jemima Boone, his frisky 14-year old daughter.

Jemima had inherited many of Daniel's traits. She didn't mean to disobey her father. But she felt she just had to follow her natural spirit, a spirit that yearned to seek and explore.

One hot July afternoon, Jemima, bored by life inside the fort, sneaked out and took a canoe onto the Kentucky River. She was with the two Callaway sisters, Liz and Frances, who were about her age.

"We felt perfectly safe," Jemima recalled later.

"Daddy had taught me how to use a canoe, and we weren't going very far."

But what the girls hadn't counted on was the river's strong undercurrent.

They nearly lost control of the canoe, and struggled to get it ashore on the far side of the river. What they didn't know was that five Indians—two Cherokees and three Shawnees—were watching them.

As soon as the girls came ashore, hundreds of yards away from the Boonesborough area, the Indians leapt out from the trees and seized them.

"No!" screamed Jemima. "Leave us be, we mean you no harm! No!" Jemima kept screaming, for Daniel had taught her to do this if she ever found herself in trouble.

But the Indian knife at Jemima's throat convinced her it was time to be silent. The Indians pushed the girls into the woods.

The Indians Leapt Out.

DANIEL BOONE

Daniel Boone was enjoying a rare mid-afternoon nap, when suddenly Dick Callaway raced into Daniel's house and shook him awake.

"The Indians have my sisters and your daughter!" Callaway screamed. "Their canoe was found ashore downstream. People heard them screaming for help!"

In only a minute Daniel was dressed and out of the house with his long rifle in hand.

"Gather up seven or eight men, tell the others to stay behind, to defend the fort," Daniel said. "Have the rest meet me by the riverbank."

As Daniel and his men began to trace the trail into the woods, Jemima and the Callaways were already several miles inland.

The three girls were frightened, hungry and thirsty. They refused to eat anything the Indians gave them. They were forced to move quickly, even though their hands were tied behind their backs.

As they moved through the woods, Jemima would purposely step down hard and break branches whenever she could, leaving a trail as her father had taught her.

They kept moving through the woods until sunset. As it grew dark, the Indians were sure that they weren't being followed and made camp for the night.

"No one's gonna save us," Frances moaned. "We'll never see our families again, if we even live!"

"We'll live," Jemima whispered. "If they were gonna kill us, they'd have done it by now."

The Indians began to laugh. Jemima tried to stay calm and confident. She knew her father was the best tracker and hunter in the world. But this might be too tough a task even for Daniel Boone.

Just then, beyond the camp area, Jemima thought she saw something move in the brush. She looked again.

Something in the Brush

Her father was staring at her! Daniel held his finger to his lips, signalling for Jemima to stay quiet. Jemima nodded slightly, so Daniel would see she understood.

Jemima glanced around. One of the Indians had fallen asleep. Three were playing some kind of game in the dirt with a stick. The other was on guard, glancing around, rifle in hand.

"Now!" came a shout from the woods, and gunfire rang out. Instantly, the Indian on guard was shot dead. Daniel and several of his men jumped out from the bushes and charged the camp area.

"Jemima, keep the girls down!" Daniel shouted.

More gunfire rang out. One more Indian fell dead to the ground. The other three escaped into the woods. Although several men gave chase, they were unable to catch them.

But that didn't matter. The kidnapping was over, and the girls were all right.

"Oh thank you, Papa, thank you, I'll never go off like that again, I promise!" Jemima cried.

"What matters is you're safe," Daniel said, as he hugged his daughter. "Mainly because you left a trail of clues we could follow. You helped save yourselves."

Daniel Boone was grateful that he hadn't lost another one of his children. But Daniel also knew what it was like when the need to explore is in your blood. He knew that Jemima would have further adventures. That's how it was on the frontier.

The group turned around and headed back to Boonesborough.

"You're Safe!"

Chapter 10

A Daring Rescue

As news of Daniel's rescue of the girls spread, his reputation grew even greater. People wanted Daniel Boone to scout land or hunt for them. With a growing family to feed, he took on as many assignments as he could.

"You can sum up all of Kentucky's wildlife in one word," Daniel was fond of saying. That word was "salt."

The Bluegrass region of Kentucky was filled with water springs that deposited layers of salt.

DANIEL BOONE

Wild animals would come to get water and lick the salt. These areas became known as "salt licks."

They were the perfect places to hunt wild game. And nobody in all of Kentucky was better at that than Daniel Boone!

On a cold February day in 1778, Daniel led a company of about thirty men out of Boonesborough and into the wilderness to hunt wild game and to collect salt for preserving food.

After the men had settled in near the frozen shores of the Lower Blue Lick, Daniel realized they would need additional food supplies. He and two other men set off to go hunting for beavers and otters.

The farther upstream they went, the colder and windier it got.

"I've never been colder in my life," said Thomas Brooks, one of the two men who had come with Daniel.

Hunting Wild Game

"Then you stay by the fire," Daniel chuckled. "I'll go upstream and lay this other trap. Wouldn't want you to get any colder, Thomas."

A grateful Brooks rubbed his hands by the campfire and watched Daniel ride off on his horse.

Daniel still loved being by himself in the open wilderness. He found it the best medicine ever invented. No matter what might ail a man, Daniel felt a trip into the open country would cure him fast.

These happy thoughts were going through Daniel's head when suddenly his horse was surrounded by four Shawnee warriors.

"Down! Now!" cried out one, holding up a tomahawk.

Daniel realized he couldn't make his horse move fast enough on the icy surface to get away. His rifle and knife were fastened to his back; he couldn't reach them. Plus, in this freezing cold, his hands were very numb.

"All right, I'll get down," Daniel said. He jumped off his horse. As soon as the first Shawnee approached him, Daniel knocked him to the ground, turned swiftly and ran off into the woods.

The others chased him. Now, Daniel was 43 years old. Although he was in fine physical condition, the Shawnees chasing him were all much younger men. After a half mile or so they were gaining on him.

Daniel realized escape was impossible. So he turned, faced his pursuers, held up his hands and surrendered.

"You are wise to surrender," a Shawnee said. "If you did not, we would kill you."

"Let us go to their camp and kill all the others!" shouted out a warrior.

Daniel thought fast. A surprise attack on the men back at the camp would wipe them out.

"Put Down Your Arms!"

"There is no need to attack them," Daniel said. "I will lead you back to the camp and we will all surrender."

The Shawnees were surprised by Daniel's offer. "All right," said the first warrior who had spoken. "We will let you lead us to your men. But if you try any tricks, I promise you will meet a swift death."

They began the trip back to the camp. On the way they met Thomas Brooks and the other hunter, who were shocked to see that Daniel, and now they, were prisoners of the Shawnees.

Soon they approached the camp. The hunters were all lying about, resting, trying to keep warm, waiting for Daniel to return. When they saw Daniel approaching, surrounded by the Shawnees, some of the men reached for their rifles.

"Put down your arms, men!" Daniel shouted. "We are surrendering to the Shawnees. I gave them my word we'd go peacefully."

The men were at first puzzled by Daniel's surrender. But when he explained that by doing this he had probably saved their lives, they understood. They would wait for the right moment when they could make their escape, Daniel quietly told them.

The men were ordered to gather up their belongings and follow the Shawnees back toward the woods.

"Where are you taking us?" Daniel asked, as they went on for several hours. It was beginning to grow dark.

"To a place you will never leave," one of them responded. The Indians all laughed. Daniel knew they were trying to frighten him. The Shawnees respected strength, not weakness.

They traveled about another three miles. Suddenly they were at a large Shawnee camp. Over a hundred warriors gathered around as Daniel was led into the center clearing.

A Large Shawnee Camp

"Who are they?" shouted one.

"Take their scalps!" shouted another.

"Burn them alive!" yelled several others.

All at once Daniel found himself face to face with Captain Will, the Shawnee chief who had captured Daniel on his earlier trip to the Appalachian Mountains.

"Captain Will!" Daniel cried out. "Good to see you again!"

Will stared at Daniel. "Do I know you?" he asked. It was at least eight years since they had met.

Daniel quickly reminded Will of their meeting in Appalachia.

"Of course!" Will boomed. "It is you, the great Long Rifle!"

Will quickly told the other warriors who Daniel was. Now the Shawnees came up to Daniel, eager to meet him and to shake his hand. All the time

Daniel was smiling. But he was looking for an opening where an escape could be made. whenever the chance came.

"Our leader wishes to see you," Will said. In moments Daniel was standing before the great Blackfish, leader of all the Kentucky Shawnees.

Blackfish was about Daniel's age. He was very stern-looking, and he was all business.

"Your hunters come to our salt licks and hunt our animals," Blackfish said. "We have spared you and these men. But we shall go to your town and kill everyone who lives there, to make sure no more of your people invade our land again!"

The Shawnees, listening, cheered and started their war chants.

Daniel knew a surprise Shawnee raid would wipe out everyone in Boonesborough. There was only one hope of saving them.

"Chief Blackfish, a raid on our town would

"Put Him to the Test!"

mean deaths for both sides," Daniel said. "It is cold now. Why not wait until spring, when I will lead you to Boonesborough, and we will peacefully turn over the entire town and fort to you."

Blackfish stared at Daniel. "Do you mean what you say?"

Daniel Boone didn't like to lie. But going back to his boyhood days, he knew that survival sometimes meant doing a small wrong for a larger good. Preventing the slaughter of Boonesborough's inhabitants was definitely a larger good.

"You have my word," Daniel replied.

"Put him to the test," shouted one warrior. "If he survives that, then he is telling the truth!" The Shawnees all cheered their approval of this idea.

Daniel swallowed hard. The Indians arranged themselves in two parallel lines. Their prisoner was then forced to run between the two lines. As he ran through, the Indians could hit him with clubs or whips, or attack him in any way they saw fit. If a man survived to the end of the line, they accepted that he was telling the truth.

Quickly the lines were formed. Though it was mid-February, Daniel was forced to strip off his shirt. Standing bare-chested, he faced the front of the lines.

"Good luck, Long Rifle," Blackfish said. "May whatever god you pray to protect you now. Begin!"

Daniel was shoved between the lines. Immediately the warriors began to scream. Daniel felt sharp whips lash across his back. A kick in the ribs knocked him down and he fell. The Shawnees laughed and taunted him. Someone kicked him again as he lay on the cold earth.

"Get up, little man, or we'll kill you here!" screamed the warrior who kicked Daniel as he was on the ground.

Suddenly, Daniel was up on his feet. He glared

A Kick in the Ribs

at the Shawnee who had kicked him. Daniel lashed out. A ferocious leg kick caught the warrior in the stomach and sent him sprawling to the ground.

The stunned Shawnees stood still in amazement. Daniel turned swiftly. He ran down the rest of the line to safety.

"Looks like I wasn't a liar!" Daniel roared. Even the Shawnee warriors had to agree.

"Well done, Long Rifle. You please me with your effort. You shall stay with us until the warmer months come, and then you will lead us to your village." Blackfish announced his decision.

So began Daniel Boone's life as a Shawnee prisoner. Although he was allowed to walk freely about and to join in the Shawnees' buffalo and turkey hunts, Daniel was always being watched. If he tried to escape he would be stopped and severely punished.

Daniel knew the Shawnees prized him above

all the others. As the weeks went by, a number of Daniel's fellow prisoners managed to escape. These escapes concerned the Shawnees, even angered them, but the one they would never take their eyes off was Daniel. All the other prisoners could escape, but as long as the Shawnees held Daniel Boone, they held the one man the settlers needed most.

What the Shawnees didn't know was that each time he went on a hunt, Daniel was secretly hiding rifle parts in a small pouch hidden inside his legging. Then, at night, he would secretly bury the parts in the ground near his sleeping area.

The winter months finally ended and spring came to Kentucky. The weather warmed, grasses and flowers grew and bloomed, and many animals roamed about. Daniel was summoned to see Black-fish.

"You have pleased me greatly, Long Rifle," the chief said. "We are adopting you into our tribe. Your

"You Are One of Us."

name shall be Sheltowee, which means rabbit. You are one of us now, my son."

Daniel took some pride in this. But he was more anxious than ever to escape, to get back to his real home, to warn his people and to see his family again. Rebecca and the children must surely think him dead by now.

"Thank you for this honor, Blackfish," Daniel said. "I will do all I can to make you proud." Then Daniel asked if he might be allowed to go out on the hunt to celebrate the honor.

It was a warm day. Daniel rode with Shawnees ahead and behind him. Suddenly a scout up front spotted a herd of buffalo in the valley below. The hunters raced off on their horses.

Daniel moved slowly. The warriors didn't know Daniel had his secret rifle wedged firmly into his leggings. This was the moment he had planned for his escape.

"Come, Sheltowee, why do you wait?" asked one warrior.

"I'm not going," Daniel replied. "I have other plans."

"You can't leave, you're one of us now!" the warrior shouted. He reached for his rifle.

But Daniel was faster. He pulled his weapon out of his legging and aimed it at the Shawnee. "I don't want to kill you, but I will if I have to," Daniel said.

The Shawnee blinked and paused. He flew off to join the other hunters, shouting "Sheltowee is escaping!"

It took Daniel over four days to find his way back. By the time he neared Boonesborough, he was weak from hunger and thirst and was nearly falling from exhaustion.

Finally, late on the afternoon of June 20, Daniel reached the entrance to Boonesborough.

Weak From Hunger and Thirst

"My word, almighty!" said the guard on duty. "It's Daniel Boone, back from the dead!"

Daniel was helped into the fort. He was fed and given help and new clothes.

But as he looked around at his fellow townspeople, Daniel saw they were glaring at him. There was no happy reaction to his return.

"Tell me, please," Daniel said, once he felt strong enough to speak. "Where is Rebecca? Where's my family?"

"Your wife and most of your family went back to Carolina two months ago, figurin' you was dead," a man responded.

Daniel nodded sadly.

"But we knew you wasn't dead 'cause about a month ago some of our scouts saw you huntin' with the Shawnees out by the salt licks. You were ridin' along with them, like you was one of 'em yourself."

"I did that to fool them into thinkin' I was one

of them," Daniel said. "To protect all of you back here."

"What you did sounds an awful lot like treason!" said the first man. The people all stared at Daniel Boone, who couldn't believe what he was hearing.

"You can't be serious!" Daniel said. "I've come back to warn you. The Shawnee are preparin' to attack us. Does that sound like treason?"

The angry stares told Daniel that the people were far from being convinced of his innocence.

"An Awful Lot Like Treason!"

Chapter 11

The Siege Of Boonesborough

Daniel knew the first thing he had to do was regain his health and strength. He had eaten very little food and had lost weight. With Rebecca and the children gone, Daniel felt sad. There was only one piece of good news; his beloved daughter Jemima had stayed on in Boonesborough.

The very next morning Daniel was summoned to appear before the Boonesborough council.

"A letter has arrived from Chief Blackfish," said Dick Callaway, head of the council. "It says that you promised the Shawnees we would turn over the fort and Boonesborough to them!"

"Yes, I said that so they wouldn't attack right away. It was meant as a way to buy time, until I could escape and come back to warn everyone," Daniel explained.

"You're a liar, Daniel Boone!" shouted one of the men. "You made a deal with the Shawnees, and when things didn't work out, you ran out on them and came back here!"

"I don't fear your trial," Daniel said. "But I greatly fear an attack by the Shawnees, which could kill us all if we're not prepared."

"Maybe all the Shawnees want is you, Boone," Callaway said. "Maybe if we give you back to them, they'll leave us alone."

A sudden scream from outside the room interrupted the argument. The men all jumped up and raced out, Daniel leading the others.

"I Don't Fear Your Trial."

"What's going on?" Callaway shouted.

"Shawnee attack is what's goin' on!" Daniel yelled as he jumped up to the top of the barricade and surveyed the scene below. Several hundred Shawnee warriors, most on horseback, had surrounded Boonesborough. They all had long rifles and knives.

"This is it!" Daniel said, leaping back down. "Grab your rifles, men, and fire for all you're worth!"

"They've got us outnumbered at least three to one!" Callaway said.

"Sounds fair to me," Daniel replied. He quickly climbed atop the barricades and began firing at the Shawnees.

Just below, Indians were trying to ram down Boonesborough's front gate. Daniel saw the danger at once.

"Men, fire at the front group only!" he shouted.

Don't let them in, or we're goners!"

All the fort's firepower came down on the group trying to break in. Within an hour, at least twenty Shawnee lay dead The rest gave up and retreated a little way.

That night the fighting ended. But Daniel knew it would only be quiet until dawn. Then it would start again.

"We've got to get reinforcements," Daniel told Callaway. "Get word to Carolina and Virginia. We need more men!"

"How many more?" Callaway asked.

"As many as they can send. And right away!" Daniel said. Daniel didn't want to alarm the others, but he knew the Shawnees better than anyone else did. And he knew the Shawnees would either conquer Boonesborough, or die trying.

After a day's fighting, the men around Daniel were exhausted. He knew they didn't have the food,

The Bullet Struck Daniel.

water, men or ammunition to hold out for long.

The siege of Boonesborough went on this way for several more days. The Shawnees fired at the fort to try to knock down the gate. The settlers fired back, and managed to keep them out.

At least thirty Shawnees had been killed. So far only one settler had died. But Daniel knew it was only a matter of time before those numbers would increase.

"Any word on the reinforcements?" Daniel asked Callaway.

"You'll know they're here when I do," Callaway replied.

"Let's hope it's sooner than later," Daniel said softly.

As Daniel turned to head back to his post, a shot rang out. A Shawnee, hiding in a tree, had taken aim and fired. The bullet struck Daniel. He fell to the ground.

"Papa!" Jemima screamed. She ran to Daniel and unwrapped his shirt.

"It's not much," Daniel said. "Just a grazing wound."

"We've killed Boone, we've killed Boone!" the Shawnee cried out from the tree.

"No you haven't, you varmint!" Daniel roared. He leaped to his feet, grabbed a rifle from a nearby soldier, aimed it, fired, and killed the Shawnee. "Now let's see who's dead!" shouted Daniel. Everyone in the fort roared.

The assault was reaching a climax. By September 17, it had gone on for eleven days. Then there was a period of calm.

"What do you think it means?" asked Callaway. "Have they given up?"

"Hardly," Daniel replied. "I'd say they're plannin' one final push to take us. If we can hold 'em off one more time, we'll have won."

"Let's See Who's Dead!"

Within an hour of Daniel's prediction, the Shawnees began a round of torching. They were throwing burning torches from the tops of nearby trees. The torches landed on top of the barricades, setting them afire.

"We've got to stop this, now!" Daniel shouted. Women and children screamed in panic as the fires blazed everywhere. Daniel had the best marksmen in the fort, himself included, climb on the barricades to fire at the Shawnees.

The attack and counterattack raged all during the rainy night and the early morning hours, but by dawn, the fires had all been put out. The Shawnees had stopped throwing the torches, and all fell silent as the rain finally stopped.

By mid-morning, as Daniel and the others scanned the countryside, there was no sign of the Shawnees.

"Open the gate," said Daniel. Cautiously, for

the first time in nearly two weeks, the men of Boonesborough went outside the walls of their town.

What they found amazed them. The Shawnees had been building an underground tunnel. They were going to burrow underneath the fort and enter Boonesborough in a sneak attack.

"And they almost made it," Daniel said, surveying the tunnel. He pointed to where the tunnel ended, only forty yards from the gate entrance.

"Why'd they stop?" one of the men said. "They were almost there."

"Last night's rain did them in," Daniel replied. "Look, it soaked the ground, turned it to mud. The entire tunnel caved in. We were lucky. When the tunnel collapsed, they knew they couldn't win. They'd had enough."

The men let out a cheer that was both of victory and relief.

"Look Who's Comin'!"

DANIEL BOONE

"Hey, look, who's that comin' over the hill?" shouted one of the men, pointing straight ahead.

Daniel squinted. It was the Army reinforcements, finally arriving from back East.

Daniel smiled. "Guess those boys need us more'n we needed them!" he roared. The siege of Boonesborough was officially over.

Chapter 12

End Of The Trail

The victory at Boonesborough was a turning point, both for Daniel personally, and the western settlements in general.

Daniel's reputation as a frontier trailblazer and fighter were now known throughout all the land.

With the Shawnee defeat at Boonesborough, it appeared the settlers might have peace.

For Daniel, who was now almost 50, that meant he might be able to spend the rest of his days

222

The Settlers Might Have Peace.

hunting in the great open frontier.

But all was not as peaceful as it seemed. By 1782 the tribes in Kentucky had regrouped for one more attack against the settlers.

Daniel and a hundred other men from Boonesborough and nearby towns were sent into the Bluegrass outback to find and destroy the Indians.

In the group was Daniel's son, Israel Boone, who was now 22 years old.

"We've lost enough of our family already," Rebecca pleaded with Daniel. "Don't let him go."

"He's a man now, he'll make his own decisions," was Daniel's reply, although deep down he wished his son would stay at home. This mission would be very dangerous. But Israel was determined to do his share, and so he came along.

Major Hugh McGary commanded the troops. The plan was to move toward the Blue Lick region to surprise and attack the Shawnees there

"They're making it easy for us," remarked McGary after just two days out. "Look at all these trail clues they're leaving."

"I think they're makin' it too easy," Daniel said, looking at all the broken branches, tobacco shavings, and other signs that littered the trail. "They *want* us to think we've discovered their trail. I think it's a trap, leading us one way, and then they'll come and attack us from another."

"Boone, you are a great trail blazer and game hunter. But I went to West Point. I give the orders. And I think I'd know a trap when I saw one."

So the unit moved on, toward the Blue Lick. A few days later they reached the river crossing. Across the way they could see a small fire smoking in a camping area.

"There it is," whispered McGary. "Okay, men, quietly across the river. Soon as we all reach the other side, on my command, we attack."

An Ambush

Daniel still didn't like it. It wasn't like the Shawnees to be this sloppy. It reminded him of the Braddock disaster.

Within twenty minutes they'd all gathered on the far side.

"Now, when I say 'charge', we head straight for that camp. Take no prisoners. I want 'em all dead," said McGary. "One, two, three, charge!"

But at that exact moment, a group of warriors numbering at least five hundred came charging out of the woods. It was an ambush!

Within two minutes, half of McGary's men had been killed. Daniel ducked behind a tree to do his shooting while the bloody battle continued.

He turned and saw young Israel standing beside him, firing his rifle. "Israel, grab a horse and git!" Daniel ordered .

"I'm no coward! As long as you stay, I stay!" shouted Israel.

DANIEL BOONE

Daniel was about to answer when there was a blast and a puff of smoke. Israel fell into Daniel's arms.

"Oh no! No! No!" shouted Daniel. He laid his son on the ground. He was dead.

As the fighting continued around him, Daniel looked around. Dazed, stunned, he dragged Israel's body out of the clearing and behind some trees.

Daniel laid down his rifle. He would have to bury a second son, lost to warfare. Daniel never wanted to fight again.

With nightfall, the battle ceased. Most of the Americans were either killed or taken prisoner.

Daniel slowly dug a grave. He placed Israel's body in it, and then covered it with soil. Daniel placed a small wooden cross, made of tree limbs, atop the grave. Then he got on his horse and returned to Boonesborough.

Over the next several years, Daniel had some

Israel Fell into Daniel's Arms.

success and some failures. He still enjoyed hunting and trapping more than anything else in the world. He and Rebecca and several of the children moved frequently in this period, but it wasn't until 1799 that the Boone family made its next big move.

At the invitation of the governor of Missouri, Daniel and the family moved to a new community on the Missouri River

"Never before have I seen hunting grounds such as these!" Daniel said to Rebecca, coming back after his first long hunt in Missouri. The beaver hunt alone provided enough money to feed the entire family for the first winter.

In the winter of 1803, Daniel was on a long hunt with a Missouri neighbor named Derry Coburn. They had caught over 50 beavers and were sitting around the early evening campfire.

"This reminds me of the good old days," Daniel said, smiling. "Just bein' out in the wilderness, no wars, no fightin', just doin' what heaven intended us to do. Nothing more and nothing less."

The words were no sooner out of Daniel's mouth than a group of a dozen Osage came storming into the camp. They shouted and screamed, raising their tomahawks and rifles.

"Yep," said Daniel. "Just like the old days."

Derry was scared, but Daniel wasn't. He knew the Indians wouldn't hurt them; all they wanted were their beaver pelts.

It was a situation Daniel had been through many times before. The only difference was these Indians also took their cooked meat, depriving Daniel of his dinner.

"Now *that's* never happened before!" Daniel shouted, as the Indians took off with their plunder.

Far worse things were about to happen to Daniel. Several more of his children died; a daughter back in Kentucky, from a mountain disease, and

"Care to Come Along?"

another daughter, there in Missouri, from a virus.

Physical problems started now, too. Daniel's old gunshot wound and various other ailments made it difficult for him to hunt or move as easily as he once did.

Then, one day, two of Daniel's friends from back in Kentucky stopped by to visit the great old man. One of them was James Bridges. "We're goin' to see the far West," Bridges said. "Far as the land will take us, till we see the ocean. Care to come along?"

It was just the medicine Daniel needed to help him heal. It was 1810 and Daniel was 76 years old. It might be his last chance ever to see the unexplored far West.

They were gone for six months. When Daniel returned home, much to Rebecca's amazement he had over 50 beaver skins. This helped pay off many past debts, with still enough left to feed the family for the year.

"How far west did you get?" Rebecca asked.

"Got to a place called Yellowstone," Daniel said. "Saw buffalo herds that from up high look like a giant brown ocean. Millions of them!"

"But you didn't see the Pacific Ocean?" Rebecca asked. She knew how much Daniel wanted to lay eyes on the great Pacific waters.

"No," he said. "That was too far. But maybe another time."

Several Missouri neighbors planned to explore the Pacific the next spring. They invited Daniel along. But the pains in his arms and legs were too great for such a journey.

Then suddenly, on March 18, 1813, Rebecca Boone died. She hadn't been sick, really. She simply went to sleep one night, and did not wake up.

For Daniel, this was the greatest loss of all. At the funeral, Daniel was too crushed even to speak.

Rebecca Boone Died.

DANIEL BOONE

After that, he never lived in his own home again. He spent time with his various children, moving from house to house.

And then, in 1817, although frail and in great pain, Daniel said he was ready to go on another long hunt. He chose as his partner his 17 year old grandson, James.

They headed into the Missouri wilderness. It was a cold January. Since Daniel, now 83, was very weak, he spent most of his time watching as James did the hunting. At night they would cook and have supper around the campfire.

"What was it like back in Carolina and Kentucky, Grandpa, when you were younger?" James asked as they ate the fresh duck they had just caught.

The campfire reflected in Daniel's eyes. "What was it like?" he chuckled. "It was very much like this. A long time ago. And very far away. But just like this."

And for Daniel Boone, there was no better feeling.

The final years of Daniel's life were spent with his children and grandchildren.

"If you can't catch 'em, you can at least cook 'em!" Daniel liked to say. Since he could no longer hunt, he insisted on cooking his dinner as often as possible, and often cooked for whichever family he was living with at the time.

Feeling ill, however, in September of 1820, Daniel wanted to have his entire remaining family with him. He traveled to where most of the family was now living, in the Missouri settlement of Femme Osage, near the Mississippi River.

When news that Daniel Boone was coming reached the town, family as well as strangers came to greet the great man.

Many of the townspeople had never seen

Daniel, only heard of him and his deeds as a frontiersman and pioneer. His reputation spanned nearly 70 years.

"All trails lead to one place, eventually," Daniel said, "and I think I have reached that place."

The next morning, on September 26, 1820, Daniel Boone died. He was one month away from being 86 years old. He was buried two days later, laid to rest in a grave beside his wife, Rebecca.

But even in death, Daniel Boone could not stay at rest. Twenty-five years later a delegation, led by some of Daniel's relatives, came to Missouri and dug up Daniel and Rebecca's graves to bring their bodies back to Kentucky.

With great ceremony, with bands playing and flags waving and people making speeches, Daniel and Rebecca Boone were reburied in Frankfort, Kentucky.

By now the legend of Daniel Boone's life had

become world-famous. He was considered the greatest frontiersman in history. His life was celebrated as an example of the new American spirit, the spirit that would win the West, though not only in the spirit of the gun or warfare. Rather, Daniel had shown that the West was a vast wilderness which, with proper care and attention, could be a land of peaceful opportunity for millions of Americans. That was the true victory.

As the coffin bearing Daniel's body was lowered on that late afternoon in Kentucky, probably nobody noticed that just as it was being placed into the ground, a shaft of sunlight broke through. It bathed the coffin in a reddish glow. A glow from the setting western sun.